Effective Inheritance Planning With Investment Property

Steve Parnham

Steve Parnham © 2019

No part of this publication may be reproduced or transmitted in any form or by any means (electronically or mechanically, including photocopying, recording or storing it in any medium by electronic means) without the prior permission in writing of the copyright owner except in accordance with the provisions of the Copyright, Designs and Patent Act 1988 or under the terms of a license issued by the Copyright licensing Agency Ltd. All applications for the written permission of the copyright owner to reproduce or transmit any part of this book should be sent to the publisher, stevesbooks@gmail.com.

Disclaimer

Please note that this book is intended as general guidance only for individual readers and does not and cannot constitute accountancy, tax, legal, investment or any other professional advice. The author accepts no responsibility or liability for loss which may arise from any person acting or refraining from action as a result of anything contained in this book.

The tax legislation and practice of HM Revenue & Customs is constantly changing and evolving. You are recommended to contact a suitably qualified tax adviser, solicitor, accountant, independent financial adviser or other professional adviser for tax, legal, accountancy, financial or other advice. Such an adviser will issue you with a letter of engagement specifically tailored to your needs and request the necessary information and details of your circumstances from you. You should also be aware that your personal circumstances will invariably vary from the general examples given in this book and that your professional adviser will be able to give specific advice based on your personal circumstances.

This book covers UK taxation and any references to 'tax' or 'taxation' in this book, unless the contrary is expressly stated, are to UK taxation only.

Contents

Preface...7

Part I - The Big Issues 10

Chapter 1 - The Issues in a Nutshell...............................11

Chapter 2 – Complete Failure: Aethelraed's Story 15

Chapter 3 – Lessons from Experience...............................27

Chapter 4 – Total Success: Alfred...................................32

Part II - Trusting Trusts...39

Chapter 5 – What History Teaches Us About Trusts...........40

Chapter 6 - Getting the Most out of Trusts 52

Part III - Planning Problems & Innovative Solutions 60

Chapter 7 – Problematic PET'S & How to Deal with Them 61

Chapter 8 – Sophisticated Planning: The Reversionary Lease 69

Chapter 9 - Sophisticated Planning: The Income Property Trust 78

Part IV - What About a Company? 86

Chapter 10 – A Company? 87

Chapter 11 - The Family Investment Company...................90

Chapter 12 - Planning in Practice 97

Chapter 13 - Discounted Share Values 103

Chapter 14 - Different Share Classes 109

Chapter 15 – Freezing Growth...111

Chapter 16 - Incorporation of an Investment Property Portfolio? ..117

Chapter 17 - Business Property Relief? 128

Part V – How to Start Planning Effectively 142

Chapter 18 - How to Start Planning Effectively 143

Thank You 150

About the Author 151

Appendix I – Tax & Formal Trusts 152

Appendix II: The Structure of Company Share Capital 156

Appendix III - Control and Management 164

Appendix IV - Asset Protection 173

Appendix V - Funding Issues for the Family Investment Company 177

Appendix VI – The Family Investment Company & Transactions in Securities 181

Appendix VII - The Family Investment Company & the Settlements Legislation 185

Appendix VIII - Information Requirements for Estate and Inheritance tax Planning 192

Preface

There are two million landlords in the UK. Between them they own 4.9 million properties with an estimated value of £989 billion. 89% of owners are individuals. Almost all of those owners and are potentially exposed to inheritance tax. That represents a lot of inheritance tax. Governments need you to pay that tax!

In the real world the blunt fact is that a stopwatch starts ticking on the day after you die. It stops just over six months later.

That is the day your family must pay the inheritance tax due on your estate. If your family needs to obtain probate, and they will where your assets include investment property, tax will be due at the time of the probate application itself.

The crucial issue for the family is therefore how on earth to pay the tax?

Inheritance tax on property can be paid by instalments over several years but most people feel that is a just a bit too much like taking out yet another mortgage in practice. Where the value of your estate is concentrated in property the result is often hasty sales to obtain the necessary funds. At a difficult emotional time, the family is also faced with impossible decisions. It is not quite the legacy they or you might have anticipated. It is not just that the estate passing to the family is significantly less than everyone thought as a consequence of the tax. It is the very practical issue of selling the family jewels or taking out loans to pay for the tax.

Most property owners will not manage the exposure to inheritance tax in their lifetime and so those who inherit their properties will suffer tax of up to 40% on the value of those properties. That means that the chance of the property business surviving intact is remote. The business will be broken up to settle the tax within just over six months of death. That is not much of a legacy!

This book tells you how to change all that.

It tells you how to pass your property business on to your successors in the most tax effective manner.

It tells you why property owners are notoriously bad at protecting their property business from inheritance tax.

It tells you why you may be stuck in a rut, endlessly poring over possibilities but never resolving anything which can be frustrating.

It gives you a highly practical series of steps to get things moving and puts you back in the same position of control as you were when you first started investing in property.

It tells you how to break free from circular thinking and secure the future of your property business.

Part I - The Big Issues

Chapter 1 - The Issues in a Nutshell

As an owner of investment property there are many good reasons why you may wish to pass those assets to the next generation at some point.

It may be part of a plan to reduce your family's exposure to inheritance tax when you depart this world.

You may not need the rental income and you may be thinking income tax and wish to take advantage of the lower tax rates that your adult children may have from an income tax perspective.

You may wish to start passing on custodianship to the next generation as part of a succession plan, particularly if you regard your investment property as a business (which it is if you are running it commercially) and not merely a random collection of assets.

All these are potentially sound reasons for planning in principle but there are usually two big downsides where chargeable assets (for capital gains tax purposes) such as property are involved.

Firstly, where your properties have increased in value since you acquired them (as you would certainly hope they will), capital gains tax will be payable on a gift of property just as if you had sold the properties to a third party. You will be gifting a valuable asset which comes with a steady income stream of immediate value to you .... but you will also be taxed on any deemed capital gain at rates of up to 28% for the privilege of doing so. That is a big step to take.

Secondly, there are asset protection issues associated with loss of control of the property. There is absolutely no protection for the gifted property once you have parted company with it.

In particular you may have concerns over young or inexperienced family members who may not have the same long term perspective or skills in property management that you have. A common worry is that beneficiaries may mortgage property or even sell it to put themselves in funds, particularly if they have expensive tastes or habits ... or might acquire them. They may also come under pressure from what you may regard as avaricious non-family members. If you no longer own the property, there is little you can do to prevent this.

Furthermore, you may prudently factor in potential claims in matrimonial or bankruptcy proceedings against the recipient of the property. The real fear here is that the beneficiary may have no choice in the matter when it comes to compromising their interest in the property. In the event of a marital breakdown the property would be an asset in any divorce settlement and its value lost in whole or in part to the family. Conversely, a failed business venture or other financial catastrophe would potentially expose a gifted property to creditors.

While the property is in your hands, you may reasonably consider that the chances of this happening are fairly remote. It is natural for you to feel that any family assets including investment property are far safer in your hands than in anyone else's. After all, you built them up and successfully managed them so why give them away and risk it all?

To achieve your objective to pass property to other family members it seems that you therefore must pay some tax upfront, possibly a great deal of tax, which is never attractive. You would be inviting a tax liability which does not otherwise need to crystallise. You must also render the assets more vulnerable to an assortment of non-family members who will have completely different agenda's to your own and may not necessarily have the overall family's interests at heart.

But is this inevitably the case?

Over the next few chapters I am going to share a couple of stories about two neighbours, Aethelraed and Alfred. Each has two investment properties which they have owned for seven years. Each property is currently worth £300,000 and each property was acquired for £100,000. Both have other assets, cash and shares, in addition to their homes. Neither of the two investment properties or the homes are subject to mortgages.

Both find that their income is sufficient to maintain their lifestyles without the rental income they currently receive from one property in isolation and each ultimately wishes to gift their property to their respective children.

Their circumstances and their concerns are identical but their outcomes could not be more different, both in terms of the taxation consequences and in terms of how future generations of the family fared. These outcomes are entirely determined by their respective mindsets and have nothing to do with their circumstances at all.

The stories of Aethelraed and Alfred are based on true stories. The family of Aethelraed pays a significant amount of tax on the two properties he owned as a consequence of doing nothing. The family of Alfred suffers no tax at all!

Their stories tell you why, how they arrive at their outcomes and how those outcomes echo down the generations!!!

Chapter 2 – Complete Failure: Aethelraed's Story

Aethelraed the unready. Admittedly, this is an unusual name for a character in a book about tax, but it is nevertheless an important and significant one. Aethelraed was king of England between 978 - 1013AD and 1014 - 1016AD. The presence of king Sweyn Forkbeard of Denmark accounts for his brief absence between 1013 - 1014 by the way.

It is tempting to believe that Aethelraed was unready in some sense but while he may well have been unready it is more an Anglo Saxon joke based on wordplay. 'Aethel' means noble in old English. 'Raed' means counsel. Aethelraed's name translates to noble counsel. The joke is that here we have a king called noble counsel who himself took no council or advice. It was what defined him. Although Aethelraed had many good advisers he would invariably take his own council. He was hapless and left his country terribly weaker than when he became king. He was not a bad man at all, in fact he was probably no better and no worse than anyone else, than you or I, but he was a poor king.

Aethelraed is most of us when it comes to inheritance tax. He is everyman. The outcome he settles for with his investment property is most peoples outcome and it is one of which HM Revenue & Customs heartily approves because they have a good chance of taking a significant cut in the value of the property on Aethelraed's death. While it is the default outcome for most people it must be recognised that as a short-term strategy it also makes a great deal of sense.

Although it had been suggested to Aethelraed that he might be well advised to consider parting company with at least one of his properties as this would reduce the inheritance tax due on his death, he decided to do nothing. His reasons for doing this are very much those set out in the last chapter … but let us look at precisely how Aethelraed thinks and acts.

Aethelraed considers gifting his property to his children as he can certainly appreciate that there is a potential issue but then learns that he faces a capital gains tax bill of just under up to £53,000 for the priviledge of doing so. He cannot do what he wishes without tax implications.

Why Capital Gains Tax?

Property and shares are chargeable assets for capital gains tax purposes.

If you sell them then a capital gain arises on the difference between the original cost to you plus enhancement expenditure and their current market value.

The first £12,000 of an individual's net chargeable gains are currently exempt (i.e. for 2019/20). The balance for investment property is taxed at 18% for gains which fall within your otherwise unused income tax basic rate band of £37,500 and 28% thereafter. The equivalent figures for commercial property are 10% and 20%. So, the actual rate depends on your overall tax circumstances.

However, if you gift a chargeable asset directly to another family member you will be deemed to have made a disposal at its market value for capital gains tax purposes even though no consideration has been received. So, the outcome is exactly the same as a sale, but you do not receive any proceeds on the transaction to pay the tax.

So how is the capital gain calculated? There are gains of £200,000 (i.e. current market value less cost) in the property against which Aethelraed could deduct the annual exemption of £12,000 if this is unused and the balance is taxed at 18%, 28% or what is sometimes called a blended rate.

A major theme of the March 2016 Budget was to differentiate between gains realised on different categories of assets. The 10%, 18% and 28% rates remained, and a new 20% band appeared alongside some seismic shifts in who is to be taxed at which rate.

The March 2016 Budget also reduced the higher rate of capital gains tax from 28% to 20%, with the basic rate falling from 18% to 10%, in relation to disposals made on or after 6 April 2016. The trust capital gains tax rate mirrored the personal higher rate reduction from 28% to 20%.

It has long been known that the optimum rate of capital gains tax is around 18%; at that level people are inclined to regard it as more of an inconvenience rather than an obstacle in considering transactions which may be chargeable to capital gains tax. The driver here therefore appears to have been to encourage investment and increase tax yields by making tax less of an issue in the context of selling investment assets. 10% is probably as good as it ever gets and no doubt some will believe that the then Chancellor went too far in reducing the basic rate.

However, amongst the types of asset that do not qualify for the reduced capital gains tax rates is residential property.

Whether one is therefore looking at the historical position or that going forward, disposing of a residential investment property will, after the annual allowance, incur capital gains tax at rates of 18% or 28% or, indeed, a blended rate where a gain straddles two tax bands. An interest in residential property includes an interest in land that has at any time in the person's ownership consisted of or included a dwelling and an interest in land subsisting under a contract for an off-plan purchase.

Inheritance Tax

Back to inheritance tax! Aetheraed does not bother to calculate the inheritance tax because he is not dead yet, indeed, he feels he has a good 20 years to go. He has written his will so that is sorted ... the properties are left to his children. What he has not made clear, perhaps because it is not really clear in his mind, is that anything left in his will is subject to the tax payable on his death. If he were to roughly calculate the inheritance tax even on the best-case scenario it should be obvious that the property is not going to pass as he intends. Nevertheless, Aethelraed feels that it is sufficient that the idea is in his head so being precise is going to be a waste of his time. His mindset ensures, indeed guarantees, that in terms of inheritance tax planning nothing will happen.

Aethelraed is also aware that doing nothing can have considerable advantages.

If he retains chargeable assets, including his properties, until he dies there is a beneficial capital gains tax effect. Although death represents a deemed disposal, no gain actually arises to his personal representatives because death is not a chargeable event. This means that the beneficiaries under his will are deemed to acquire the relevant assets at their then market value or probate value at no tax cost. Death therefore effectively washes out any inherent historical capital gains built up during his lifetime for the family. Where your family inherit assets on death and those assets have significantly grown in value under your stewardship, that growth in value can effectively be realised by them free of capital gains tax if assets are disposed of fairly shortly after your death.

What does Aethelraed do?

Having briefly looked at the capital gains tax implications we can now return to Aethelraed's dilemma and see what he does in practice.

Aethelraed understands that the potential capital gains tax charge means that if he wishes to gift a property he must draw on his vital cash savings which is not an attractive prospect. While he is perfectly happy to give up the income on one property he struggles with the idea of having to pay capital gains tax as well. In fact, if he were completely honest with himself, he actually quite likes the financial cushion the rental income gives him and is loathe to lose that sense of security. While it has been suggested to him by a professional adviser that the gain could be deferred Aethelraed feels that this would not suit him either. Why? No one ever found out. It was just a feeling.

He procrastinates, decides not to decide, and does nothing. However, Aethelraed does from time to time revisit the looming threat of inheritance tax but his eternal reflections do not lead him to take action. At least he hasn't incurred a tax liability up front and the property is still very much under his protection. He has no focus on the more distant future, a future where it is the family rather than himself who will suffer the tax consequences. He will never see the practical consequences of his decision.

Although he constantly resurrects the idea of mitigating inheritance tax no practical steps are undertaken and Aethelraed dies 18 years later. Being a pessimist, Aethelraed assumed that property prices would remain fairly flat during the remainder of his lifetime and, had they done so, his property would suffer £120,000 inheritance tax on this property alone, leaving a mere £180,000 for the family who may be forced to consider a sale of one property to fund the tax liability.

Effectively Aethelraed has traded a £53,000 capital gains tax liability for a £120,000 inheritance tax liability. Well over double the tax! Aethelraed took the view that he had not incurred the capital gains tax liability in his lifetime and so has preserved his legacy. The inheritance tax is not his problem.

There is a silver lining too. The son he was intending to give the property to was involved in a messy divorce. As the son did not own the property his former wife's divorce lawyers were not able to bring the value of the property into account in the settlement.

Considering the lack of capital gains tax and the divorce Aethelread was convinced that he had made good solid decisions which were in his and the family interests. The time for reflection, which had consumed most of Aethelraed's life, was over.

Aethelraed passes away confident that all is well....and from his extremely limited perspective he is right.

Why Inheritance Tax?

At present inheritance tax is payable at a single rate of 40% on death where the value of your total assets and less liabilities together with the value of any chargeable gifts made in the seven years prior to death exceeds £325,000. The first £325,000 of an individual's estate is therefore liable to inheritance tax at 0%. This is known as the nil rate band.

Each individual has a nil rate band. Any portion of an individual's nil rate band which is unused on death is transferrable to a surviving spouse or civil partner where relevant for use on the second death. In addition, transfers between husband and wife during their lifetimes are exempt from inheritance tax. Consequently, inheritance tax tends to be a tax which falls on the second death of a married couple since most couples leave their estate to the survivor.

For inheritance tax purposes a gift to an individual in lifetime represents a potentially exempt transfer or PET. There is no inheritance tax when the gift is made, and a charge would only arise where you died within seven years of making the gift. When an individual makes an outright gift, the basic inheritance tax position is that the gift is a potentially exempt transfer. Accordingly, if the person who has made the gift survives for seven years, the gift will be free of inheritance tax.

A form of tapering relief is available where a donor dies at least three years after making the gift. This relief reduces the inheritance tax payable but not the value transferred. The relief is given on a sliding scale from 20% relief where death occurs between three - four years after the gift to 80% where we are looking at years six - seven.

. . . .

Aethelraed's story vividly illustrates the inherent contradiction with respect to the capital gains tax and inheritance tax aspects of the equation.

In many ways the perfect capital gains tax strategy is to hold onto your assets until you die so that the family can obtain these at their then market value for tax purposes. Any future sales will take their cost for purposes of calculating gains as the market value at the date of your death. Exactly as Aethelraed did.

This is not, of course, an efficient strategy from an inheritance tax perspective as the full market value of the assets will be taxed at 40%, subject to your available nil rate band(s).

It is particularly ineffective where the family has no intention to sell the property at all, as was the case for Aethelraed's family.

The Sting

There is a massive sting in the tail for Aethelraed's family, however.

In reality Aethelraed's decision to do nothing has cost the family much more than £120,000 because the value of the property didn't remain stable since making the gift. He had held it for 25 years by then, 18 years after his deliberations, and its value had doubled taking its market value to £600,000 and increasing the inheritance tax liability to £240,000 compared to a capital gains tax liability of £53,000 at the time of the potential gift. Aethlraed's executors prudently obtained two probate valuations at the time and both were in the region of £600,000. His decision had cost his family almost five times the tax he would have paid had he transferred the property years before. And that was before considering the other property which would suffer comparable tax liabilities. A play around on something like the Nationwide's House Price Calculator will confirm that house prices have indeed increased over certain periods of time by considerably more than 100%.

The family are even more questioning of the legacy when they find out that Aethelraed could have gifted the property without even paying the £53,000 capital gains tax. That is exactly what Alfred did!

Before feeling too much sympathy for Aethelraeds family, it must be acknowledged that the family, of course, did go along with Aethelraed's strategy of doing nothing at the time. As in many comparable circumstances, the family took the easy option of, "We are not interested in your money. You enjoy it while you can". While that may be a non-contentious short term attitude to adopt (as indeed is that of Aethelraed himself), it is rarely an effective one where taxation is concerned. The reality is that both Aethelraed and his family did not choose plan for the inevitable and entirely predictable inheritance tax liability. They were all stuck in their relatively restricted comfort zones. Aethelraed's family only became focussed on the value of the estate when they truly appreciated the consequences of everyone's inactivity ... and by then it was far too late to consider remedial action. The inheritance tax was due for payment six months after the end of the month of Aethelraed's death so there is little time to think clearly at an emotional time.

Running a business but deferring what amounts to easily the biggest expense of that business until six months after you die is unlikely to result in the business remaining intact for the family. It is also astoundingly poor business management. You do not get to see the damage but the expense is so massive that it effectively breaks the business for the new owners. Assets need to be sold off to settle it. It is possible, as already mentioned, to settle the liability over ten years but it is just a little too much like saddling the new owners with a ten-year mortgage plus interest on 40% of the value of the business. A tainted legacy and a questionable business strategy!

Chapter 3 – Lessons from Experience

Before we turn to Alfred, I should like to consider four principles or axioms which, in my experience, underpin successful inheritance tax planning for property. Taken in the round they constitute an effective mindset.

My professional experience has taught me that the people who are most successful at limiting their exposure to inheritance tax are those who exhibit to some extent four characteristics. Those four characteristics are more fully explained in my companion book, 'The Absolute Essence of Inheritance Tax Planning' Chapter 7 but by way of a short introduction I will set them out here.

I was never taught those principles professionally and never seen them set out in written material. That is not surprising. Writers on these matters tend to be technically focussed and are almost exclusively concerned with how much tax can be saved but it is more complex than that. Inheritance tax is often a tax which taxpayers will not easily see for themselves and so it can be a hard sell for advisers. People are naturally nervous about something which is poorly explained and coloured by emotion and unspoken assumptions. Whether it makes sense depends on how comfortable they feel.

Axiom One: Life is uncertain.

The successful appreciate that life can be uncertain and unpredictable. It therefore makes sense to take that into account in planning one's affairs. It is all very well assuming that you will live indefinitely or even for the more modest next seven years ... but don't bank on it. However young you are. Aethelraed knew he was mortal but....

Axiom Two: Be in it for the long term.

Inheritance tax planning is a long-term issue and being long-term enables the owners of investment property to put together a strategy which they follow, and family members follow. The senior members ensure that it is enforced with an almost military discipline. There are no exceptions or excuses or indulgences from that duty. There is no thought of doing only what one is inclined to do. One either accepts the party whip on this or you will be side-lined. The ability to operate with this mindset can confer quite extraordinary power and confidence.

By the same token, if the founder of a property business is only inclined to go through the motions and doesn't take things seriously it is no surprise that this will also be the mindset of the wider family. Compare the outcome to those (often landed or aristocratic) families that have preserved their family wealth over generations, hundreds of years. Look at the mindset. There is no comparison!

Axiom Three: Family not Individual

The successful are focussed on 'how the family preserves those assets' not 'how do I preserve them'. Not what is in it for me but custodianship for the family.

Axiom Four: The Nature of the Assets

It is often the nature of the assets and how their owner regards those assets which determines how successful they are in their planning endeavours. Those who are interested in inheritance tax mitigation instinctively focus on just that, but it is often quite difficult for them or their professional adviser to generate enthusiasm when all they are looking at is a bunch of assets, albeit very valuable ones, including cash, chattels and shares. Does it really matter whether a family member gets X amount rather than Y amount with the difference being the tax? Probably not if it is just cash.

The vital difference between the successful and those who are less so lies in the idea of succession, of leaving property or a business such that it can survive you and benefit your family. A legacy in other words

If you combine these four axioms as you consider your circumstances your planning will stand a much, much better chance of success. In fact, all successful inheritance tax planning exhibits these principles to a greater or lesser degree.

By contrast Aethelraed had a short-term perspective, a bit like the annual tax returns he was used to submitting. He rather liked his surplus income, he could not let his property go and he was shy of paying more tax or even further professional fees. Indeed, he had left his previous accountant because he thought that he was paying too much even though he was never charged for the pitiful but time consuming inheritance tax advice he had received. It demonstrates that he did not value that advice. He saw it as worthless or just worth a few pounds.

You may not have to think in terms of 500 or 1,000 years like the landed aristocracy but you can and must think in terms of ten or twenty years. You may not have to think of many generations of family, indeed perhaps future generations should have responsibility for their own planning and take that custodianship as seriously as you do, but you may well think of your living family before, "What's in it for me ?"

Now we must turn to Aethelraeds neighbour, Alfred. The legacy he left would have repercussions down the generations of his family.

Chapter 4 – Total Success: Alfred

Alfred is in exactly the same position as Aethelraed and, just like Aethelraed, would probably not make the gift of property if it meant liquidating his other investments and suffering capital gains tax on these disposals. It is a real concern. But he had an open mind. Unlike Aethelraed, he decides that he needs to take action on the grounds that he wishes his son to be his successor. However, he does not give the property directly to his children because he wished to minimise, if not eliminate, both capital gains tax and inheritance tax on his entire estate. Instead he transfers the property to a trust with his children as beneficiaries.

The advantages of gifting the property to a trust over gifting to an individual are threefold for Alfred:

Firstly, it addresses Alfred's worry about losing control. Alfred keeps control even though ownership of the asset has changed. The trustees are in a decisive position to control the assets within the trust subject to the wording of the trust deed. The potential for asset protection is consequently unsurpassed. Alfred remains in control of the trust assets indefinitely by being the first named and lead trustee. The trustees have maximum flexibility since the settlor, Alfred, designates the class of beneficiaries amongst whom the trustees have absolute discretion as to how they deal with both the income and capital. The assets are going nowhere without Alfred's consent.

Secondly, the complication of a capital gains tax liability crystallising where chargeable assets are gifted is where a formal trust comes into its own. Unlike the case with an absolute gift to an individual, capital gains tax holdover relief is available with the consequence that there is no tax at all to pay on the gift and the children, as beneficiaries of the trust, take over the property at its original base cost of £100,000.

Thirdly, and by a strange coincidence, Alfred's son subsequently becomes divorced. As Alfred no longer owns the property can the solicitor acting for his ex-wife bring the property into the divorce settlement? Absolutely not. The trustees have a duty to protect the assets under trust law and under the terms of the trust deed. They will resolutely and successfully resist anything along these lines.

In my experience trustees are tenacious in defending their trust because not to do so could have unfortunate consequences for them personally.

So, how does the holdover relief work?

Capital Gains Tax Again: Holdover Relief

To holdover means to defer. But defer until when? Until the new owner sells the property to a third party if, indeed, they ever do. If you can holdover a gain this means that you can gift it without paying capital gains tax yourself.

The capital gain on investment assets, including most property and shares, cannot usually be held over but there is one crucial exception – where the assets are gifted to a relevant property trust. The capital gains tax on such gifts can be deferred on the grounds that they are potentially subject to a lifetime inheritance tax charge and, without the ability to defer the capital gains tax, there would be a double charge to tax. That currently remains the case even though no inheritance tax may be payable in practice because the gift is within the donor's nil rate band of, at the time of writing, £325,000.

For capital gains tax purposes, any gain arising on the transfer of chargeable assets into trust can be held over or deferred without limit. You would not need to pay any capital gains tax now or in the future on creating the trust. A huge advantage given the inherent gains in many property portfolios!

if the transfer is within the inheritance tax nil rate band there will not be any inheritance tax payable either. Where a disposal made by an individual or trustees is a chargeable transfer for inheritance tax, then capital gains tax holdover relief is available on the gain.

Holdover relief is therefore a way to put off paying capital gains tax until the new owner of the asset, the trustee, sells it.

It is necessary to advise HM Revenue & Customs of the details and fortunately this can be achieved by completing and submitting a straightforward form HS295 available from the HM Revenue & Customs website. The form needs to be signed and dated by the person transferring the property into trust and by the trustees who accept the asset. Certain information such as the date of disposal will need to be entered on the form. There is also an opportunity to defer any valuation by HM Revenue and Customs.

You need to get the paperwork right and obtain accurate information, but the prize is that the donor does not need to pay capital gains tax on transferring the property to the trust. It is not a PET though. It is a chargeable lifetime transfer.... though a transfer which is chargeable at a rate of 0% because it is within the transferor's available nil rate band.

Back to Alfred !

This means that if, for example, Alfred transfers his property worth £300,000 to his new trust, the gain of £200,000 will be held over until, and indeed if, the trustees ever dispose of the asset. So, if the trustees eventually sell the property for £600,000, they will have to pay capital gains tax on a gain of £500,000 consisting of their own gain of £300,000 plus the held over gain of £200,000. In other words, the gain of £200,000 is deferred until the ultimate sale.

What is happening here is that the trustees take over the original capital gains tax cost of the asset and hence the potential liability on its subsequent disposal and with HM Revenue and Customs accepting that no gain arises on the transfer to the trust.

Alfred transfers the property to a trust for his children and dies 18 years later and the property suffers no inheritance tax charge as it is no longer in his estate. He doesn't own it.

So how does the inheritance tax side of the trust work?

The Relevant Property Trust

What is less often appreciated is that the property doesn't have to remain in the trust indefinitely. The trustees may decide that the beneficiaries should take possession of the property after a few years and a further holdover claim using the form HS295 form could be made to ensure that, once again, no capital gains tax is payable on the transfer from trustees to beneficiaries.

A relevant property trust is effectively treated as a separate person for inheritance tax purposes and provides an opportunity to shelter assets within a vehicle which exists outside of an individual's estate without losing control or paying tax on the transfer.

A transfer of assets to a relevant property trust is potentially subject to an immediate lifetime charge to inheritance tax and accordingly you would be unlikely on these grounds to settle more than £325,000 worth of assets each into such a trust every seven years because of the likelihood of a lifetime charge of 20% arising on the excess.

Any amount up to that value will be covered by Alfred's unused inheritance tax nil rate band.

To be effective for inheritance tax purposes however, Alfred and his minor children cannot benefit from the trust in any way. Although he cannot benefit from the fund personally, there is of course a real advantage to Alfred insofar as the fund could, say, meet the expenses of his adult children or grandchildren that he might otherwise meet out of his personal income.

Where there are significant inherent capital gains in your property you may wish to transfer, then a relevant property trust is a MUST because the capital gains can be ignored.

The only real downside is that there is a relatively low ceiling on the value which can be transferred into the trust every seven years without triggering a lifetime inheritance tax charge. i.e. £325,000.

Trusts are inevitably subject to their own tax regime and this is set out in a little more depth in appendix I.

So how did it all turn out?

Alfred's son inherited the property without inheritance tax on Alfred's death and his experience of the events which led to that outcome opened his eyes to the possibility of establishing his own property business. That is the real legacy. It is not financial, it is a mindset akin to the one adopted by landed families throughout history to preserve family assets as a custodian.

Part II - Trusting Trusts

Chapter 5 – What History Teaches Us About Trusts

The reasons Alfred embraced the idea of a trust are straightforward. He had the mindset. His professional adviser, though not a specialist, took the time to properly explore the taxation implications of the trust. That was sufficient but what I have never seen or heard a professional adviser do is to take the time to explain how the concept of the trust originated. It is very enlightening.

It is also very surprising because knowing where trusts originated from gets to the very heart of what they are used for in the 21st century in a way that merely dryly stating and re-stating facts can never do. It brings colour to a black and white picture and increases the chance that the reader 'gets it'.

In another sense it is not surprising. Most private client tax practitioners are technically focussed and can send you to sleep with their musings on exactly which clause to use in a deed ... and rightly so. It is they who will have to implement the trust. Also, it is quite likely that they may simply be unaware of the origins. It is a great shame because trusts have been used for estate planning and asset protection for centuries, and their usefulness and flexibility for these purposes have been proven by the test of time. The origin of trusts can be traced back to two prominent sources in medieval times and is valuable to look at them partly to see how they originated but also to appreciate that they emerged against the background of addressing some very crucial needs. They did not magically appear for no reason. Nor have they endured for no reason.

While trusts have evolved over the years, the principle behind them remains pretty much the same. Centuries later we still use them just as our ancestors did, for the preservation of family wealth. The eternal problem which trusts addressed is that throughout history and left to their own devices people who did not own a particular piece of land, those in power, were intent on taking it or at least a significant cut in it for their own purposes and wellbeing. Sound familiar?

The Crusaders

The big problem for crusaders was that they couldn't take their land with them. They had to leave it behind no matter how many years they were away and that meant that their land was potentially vulnerable to the avaricious and unscrupulous.

The attractions of going on crusade were however not inconsiderable. In a supposedly more pious age, a participant could look forward to being forgiven their past sins. In circumstances where your eternal soul was paramount that attraction cannot be underestimated. For those of a more worldly nature it was also possible to avoid paying interest on debts while ostensibly in the service of the church. If you had considerable debts a period of temporary 'debt-forgiveness' could be an absolute life saver. Some were also attracted by a new start elsewhere although many intended to return.

If the intention was to return from the crusades, then your big issue was to find someone trustworthy to look after your estate for you in your absence. Unfortunately, common law gave no assistance here. Although effective in many circumstances it was simply not subtle enough to deal with this sort of situation.

So, to address this matter when a landowner left his home in, say, England for the crusades, he would convey the ownership of his land to a trusted acquaintance, literally a trustee. The trustee would manage the estate and pay and receive feudal dues on the crusader's behalf, on the understanding that ownership would be conveyed back to the crusader on his return. Approaching someone to hold your land in trust would in principle protect your assets from all manner of potential usurpers in your absence.

Unfortunately, when presented with temptation human nature is often found wanting and this was equally so in earlier times.

Returning crusaders could encounter refusal from the trustee to hand over the property and, regrettably for the crusader, English common law did not recognise the claim; as far as the King's courts were concerned, the land now belonged to the trustee who was under no particular obligation to return it. The crusader had no legal claim. As returning crusaders were to discover, common law would regard a change of ownership as effectively relinquishing all their claims to the property.

An easy sting then but someone like a battle-hardened crusader would hardly take what amounted to theft of everything he held dear lying down. The crusader in his frustration would petition his king, who would in turn refer the matter to the Lord Chancellor. The Lord Chancellor would decide the result of the case according to his conscience. The Lord Chancellor invariably considered it unacceptable that the legal owner (the "trustee") could go back on his word and deny the claims of the crusader (the "true" owner). He would therefore usually find in favour of the returning crusader. Hurrah! That makes sense.

The common law rules of the time provided a satisfactory and a fair solution to most issues, controversies and disputes but it was equity which established that a trust is a relationship whereby property is held by one party for the benefit of another.

Equity would look at the overall circumstances and recognise that the transfer to a trustee was on a time limited basis and so it was that the idea of equity as a legal principle began to emerge around this time.

These conceptual advances were established early in medieval England but may have come to nothing had there not been even earlier and deeper forces at work. By the end of the 13th century the crusades had fizzled out but those earlier and deeper forces were throwing up unsustainable contradictions in the way society was ordered. The 14th century was to witness a radically different way of dealing with property which flows down to the present time.

The Law of Inheritance

To see those forces at work we need to go back even further in time to the immediate aftermath of the Norman conquest. William, now William I of England, gave parcels of land to those who had supported him in his audacious gamble. His supporters did the same and so on further down the chain with the king as technical owner of last resort. Everyone, save the king, was effectively a tenant. In return for the land granted down this chain came a corresponding obligation to provide services. In fact, the whole of society was based on the rights and obligations surrounding the holding of land which represented the beginning of feudalism.

This worked fine as a system when you had a relatively small military elite dominating the civilian population but by the beginning of the 13th century a market economy was beginning to emerge and so the implicit bargain of services for land was slowly starting to break down and fade away. Many forms of service were being commuted to cash rents and ultimately cash became the price for land. Everyone really preferred cash to services and, crucially, this fundamental change was umbilically linked to the idea of inheritance.

Under the feudal system when a tenant died his land passed to his heir, provided that certain niceties (another word for tax) were complied with. This essentially meant that there was potentially a lot of cash to be realised on the death of a tenant for the king and lesser landlords. It was not possible to make a will for land in those days before the owner died. If you could achieve this, it would represent excellent planning because the feared indents of tenure would not be due.

The problem in dying while still owning your land was twofold:

Firstly, the imposition of customary feudal incidents, the payment of feudal relief on an inheritance, the temporary loss of control of a fiefdom a through wardship where the landholder was under the age of majority, and the forcible marriage of a young heiress. The land-holding escheat could revert permanently to the overlord, as was customary where the land-holder died without a legal heir.

Secondly, the landholder was bound by the custom of primogeniture where the eldest son alone had the right, on payment of the appropriate feudal relief of course, to inherit even in circumstances where that is not appropriate.

What had started out as a stitch up by an occupying power with everyone at the top benefitting had now become the defining characteristic of a system which no longer delivered for almost everyone but the king. For everyone below the king it meant families suffering hefty taxes on the death of the head of the family and from being unable to direct the land effectively to the next generation. They were looking at a succession tax paid to a lord by the heir of a deceased person to effect transfer of property and rights between generations. Again, sounds familiar?

A remedy was needed to allow society and an increasingly market economy to move forward. The only way around it was to divest oneself of the land before you died so that the infamous 'incidents of tenure' were not due on death. The tenant would therefore give his land to several people with the explicit direction that the land should be given to the chosen one or ones after the tenant's death. The practice of passing land to a group of trusted friends or relatives or other allies while retaining use of the lands, began to be widespread by the mid to late 1300's thus solving both problems simultaneously.

But what does this mean for us?

Tenants (which could include powerful landed families as well as those with just a few fields) would use trusts to keep their lands intact and to ensure that they devolved to the family member who was best suited to lead that family in the long term. That is not necessarily the elder son as dictated by primogeniture.

Once the trust had been established the death of the beneficial owner was legally irrelevant to its continued holding by the trustees. The trustees simply allowed the lands to continue to be used by the deceased's heir. The feudal overlord, and ultimately the king himself, was not entitled to exact feudal relief from the new beneficiary. The effect was that on a man's death he appeared to hold little or no land, while in reality he had full use of it and of the revenues derived from it. One could characterise this as tax avoidance. One could also see it as a way of releasing an implacable obstacle to a market economy stifled by the rigidities of a feudal order which was becoming less relevant on an annual basis. A matter of perspective then.

Legal title no longer passed by succession and landowners were able effectively to bequeath land to whomsoever they wished.

However, giving your land to someone on the basis of trust alone was a little flimsy as the crusaders had discovered. Equity was based on what a good conscience should do. If individuals were asked to hold land for someone else equity holds that they should not be allowed to renege on that agreement as happened under the crusades. Consequently, the Court of Chancery began to manage such trusts and by the 1400's trust work took up most of the Courts time. The principle which had been established in the previous century now began to come into its own with trusts becoming recognised as a legitimate approach to organising one's affairs.

The crusades and the desire to avoid the duty of inheritance together spurred on the expansion of trusts. Both crusaders and anyone in the feudal vassal-lord relationship required a mechanism to avoid the consequences their land would suffer under common law. Both were ready to trust others in ways that were far too subtle for common law to appreciate.

Aethelraed & Alfred

Alfred never looked at planning from the angle of whether he liked something or not. Life had taught him that this approach would only indulge his prejudices and provide excuses for doing nothing or procrastination. The only question for Alfred was whether a trust could help him achieve his objectives. Insofar as a trust would allow him to ignore the capital gains tax charge there was no doubt in his mind that it would help him. It was a purely practical and business driven decision. He was also prepared to take advice and would delegate the actual implementation to specialists. Aethelraed would delegate little.

Aethelraed had certainly considered trusts in a 'box ticking' way as was implied in chapter 2 and while he took on board the possibility of holdover relief the reality is that he never actually 'got' the concept at all. Consequently, it was always going to be a non-starter for him. The possibility was snuffed out for him and his family when he concluded that 'he didn't like trusts'. In this he was nowhere near as sharp as those guys back in the 1300's and indeed everyone who has planned over the last 600 – 700 years. To dismiss an idea with such a long and proven history and one of success is an act of personal indulgence and nothing more. It is something that can only be countenanced by someone who does not have the mindset revealed in chapter

3 and who cannot think beyond personal gain in one's lifetime. Not liking something is just an excuse for doing what you please.

Aethelraed never really had it explained to him though. His adviser had briefly said that there were opportunities to holdover the gain into a trust in the right circumstances but this did not make an impact since the adviser knew little about trusts and certainly would not want to advise on their implementation. To be fair it would have made no difference in practice since Aethelraed was wedded to the day to day running of his letting business, which he felt would die with him. Something which took a long-term perspective would seem woolly and vague and far, far away for him. Aethelraed was also used to regular though modest professional fees for his annual tax return and accounts and felt that a trust was just an attempt to rack up fees unnecessarily. He would have been better to ask whether his adviser, who was fantastic at preparing returns, accounts and the day to day running of the business, had the right mindset for this work and was comfortable with long term estate planning. That neither Aethelraed or his adviser had the mindset and that neither had detailed and accurate information at their fingertips on the properties is guaranteed, yes guaranteed, to lead nowhere.

The real question here is why you are not using trusts. They have developed to represent a major planning tool in the 21st century and the concerns they address are very, very similar to those which gave rise to the early trusts – protecting assets for the family against all manner of threats including punitive taxation.

Chapter 6 - Getting the Most out of Trusts

Where people use trusts, they will generally just accept them at face value and once created they are forgotten. That amounts to getting about 25% value from the core idea. The trust needs to be a part of your life and your life and you need to really engage with it to get the other 75%, as was the case with our ancestors. Taking the basic principle further one can consider quite a high level of fine tuning.

Married Couples & Civil Partners

Our two stories in chapters 2 and 4 assumed for simplicities sake that Aethelraed and Alfred were unmarried or were widowers. Suppose each was happily married or were in a civil partnership. On this assumption they could have doubled the value of the property which could be placed into trust at any one time.

This is because each individual has a nil rate band as noted earlier. If husband and wife were both to separately establish such a trust, up to £650,000 could be removed from their joint estates after seven years, representing a maximum inheritance tax saving of £260,000. You could continue to do the same every seven years if that were practical to maximise the use of the two nil rate bands.

Transfers between spouses are capital gains tax and inheritance tax free so it is possible to make inter-spouse gifts prior to the recipient making a later gift tax free where one spouse has most of the wealth.

If married, Aethelraed or Alfred could have passed, say, 50% of the properties to their spouse or civil partner and made gifts of a proportion of the property to children to take advantage of the capital gains tax annual exemption. The gains on the first property are £200,000 so using the joint annual exemptions would reduce the time taken to pass the property without capital gains tax charge from 17 years to about nine years but would still have to wait several years before it was out of the estate for inheritance tax purposes. If the gain had risen to £500,000 as happened for Aethelraed and Alfred in practice, they would be looking to reduce a potential 42 year wait to 21 years using this strategy.

Using a trust ensures, however, that the property could be gifted in one go and within seven years the value would be out of the inheritance tax net.

Individuals may consider marriage or civil partnership a useful form of inheritance tax planning but that would only be the case if circumstances permitted. And comes with some caveats. It is not consequently recommended on these grounds alone.

The Annual Exemption.

Everyone has an annual exemption of £3,000.

If one assumes that both of the 2019/20 annual exemptions of £3,000 remain unused as well as those for 2018/19 in respect of a married couple, the initial contribution into the trust could be increased to £331,000 each. If payments up to the annual exemption were made in each of the subsequent six years this would increase the payments in by a further £18,000 to £349,000 each. A joint contribution to the trust would increase the total transferred in this way from £650,000 to £698,000.

Growth

Even if you do not survive the gift by seven years, gifting regularly remains a good strategy for rapidly appreciating assets. Alfred understood the potential for growth over the coming decade or two in a way that Aethelraed could not. His main objective was therefore to place that growth outside of his estate. Although the value of the gift was £300,000 when made, when he died it was worth £600,000. That is a £240,000 tax saving with no capital gains tax implications. The value taken in to account is the value on transfer rather than on death.

If you do survive for seven years, even better!

Loans

Our two stories assumed for simplicities sake that Aethelraed and Alfred held properties which were free of mortgages. When a property is transferred to a trust and is also subject to a mortgage, for inheritance tax purposes the value of the transfer is the net value rather than the value of the unencumbered property. This presents a useful opportunity for considerably greater flexibility in inheritance tax planning. If all your properties are held without loans, then there is scope to borrow to reduce the lifetime inheritance tax charge on the property on the transfer into trust. While this offers a strategy to pass greater value represented by property into trust without inheritance tax, there is a limit to the approach. This limitation arises from the deeper capital gains tax implications, particularly in relation to the essential capital gains tax holdover relief on transfers into trust. The issue is that for capital gains tax purposes any mortgage assigned to the trust will be deemed to represent consideration paid for the property transferred to the extent it exceeds cost. Why is that an issue?

Any excess over the cost of the property will be deemed to represent consideration and becomes, as a consequence, immediately chargeable for inheritance tax purposes. It is not possible to hold over any part of the gain that would have arisen on a sale of the property for the amount of this deemed consideration. Furthermore, where the deemed consideration represented by the mortgage exceeds £125,000 stamp duty land tax (SDLT) will become payable.

The point is to utilise loans only up to the acquisition cost of the property and any enhancement cost to reduce inheritance tax and then either spend the funds or give away the equity released as a PET. As always this requires really excellent records.

A potential solution would therefore be to arrange to mortgage the property prior to the transfer and assign the loan to the trust. This will reduce the property's net equity value at the time of transfer and thus reduce or eliminate the inheritance tax charge.

Gift a Share of a Property

A gift of property into trust does not necessarily have to be a full 100% interest. It could be a proportion of it. The advantage of doing this is threefold.

Firstly, where property values are relatively high, a transfer of 100% of the property to a trust may trigger a lifetime inheritance tax charge where its value exceeds the inheritance tax nil rate band. A part transfer of, say, 50% may give greater flexibility where this is a concern.

Secondly, there may sometimes be an interesting inheritance tax advantage. Where a property is jointly owned with someone who is not the deceased person's spouse, it is usually possible for executors to argue for a reduction in the value of the deceased person's share when working out the deceased's liability to inheritance tax. Generally, this is accepted to be a reduction of about 10% to reflect the difficulty in selling a jointly owned share of a property and where the value of a joint owner's share may be reduced because the other owner has the right to keep living in the property.

Where property is jointly owned with a trust, it may consequently be possible for the executors to argue for a reduction in the valuation in the right circumstances and therefore of the inheritance tax especially if the executors and trustees are different people.

Thirdly, a partial gift of a property opens the possibility of retaining 100% control but nevertheless allowing some value to pass from your estate. You might gift a third of a property for instance and retain two-thirds. Any independent action with respect to the one third share is very much constrained and, indeed, there is nothing to stop the two thirds share entering a formal trust.

Did Alfred do all this?

No. His was a simpler situation but, he did decide to create a new trust seven years and the value of the property initially going into his first trust did indeed double in value from that date. The result was that he paid no capital gains tax on setting the trust up and paid no inheritance tax on both the value of the assets when they went in or the growth in those assets on his death.

Alfred, as we have seen, simply saw trusts as a means to an end. It was immaterial whether he liked them or not. If they helped him to achieve is aim then they were useful, really useful. If they did not help, then they were not useful. So it would have been in 1375. The answer has been waiting for Aethelraed for 700 years, but he cannot see it. For Alfred it has been maturing for 700 years and it was made for him.

Alfred was intent on transferring a business to his children. Aethelraed was just aiming to save tax and professional fees, do it at compliance rates with respect to professional fees and without any inconvenience to himself. Property was simply something he did. Totally different mindsets with totally different outcomes.

Even small landowners in the 1300's simply would not have understood Aethelraed.

In the medieval period it became established that it is possible to separate legal and beneficial ownership and that anyone holding property to which they are not beneficially entitled have both rights and obligations as trustees. A trustee could not use the camouflage of common law to mask deceit and dishonesty, for instance. It was a crucial development in estate planning and one which continued down into the 21st century.

Part III - Planning Problems & Innovative Solutions

Chapter 7 – Problematic PET'S & How to Deal with Them

When the government introduced inheritance tax back in 1984 these were happy days. The legislation in Inheritance Act 1984 is a model of clarity and is undoubtedly a fine example of what legislation should strive to be. There was a huge omission, however. Before 17 March 1986, it was possible to make a gift that was effective for inheritance tax purposes even if the donor continued to receive some benefit in the asset given away. This was a major flaw in the Inheritance Tax Act 1984 and very quickly Finance Act 1986 was introduced to put a stop to this loophole by introducing new rules, similar to those that operated for estate duty, and designed to make sure that such assets would still be treated as part of the donor's estate for inheritance tax purposes.

These rules are known as the gifts with reservation rules. Such gifts are often referred to by the acronym GROB or GWR.

A GWR is, broadly, a gift of property made by an individual on or after 18 March 1986, whereby either the recipient does not enjoy possession of the gifted property, or the donor continues to enjoy or benefit from it; if there is a reserved benefit within seven years of the donor's death then the gift is caught by the

GWR rules. The effect is that the gifted property is treated as part of the donor's estate for inheritance tax purposes. This could potentially result in the same gift being taxed twice though there are provisions which provide relief in those circumstances.

If the reservation of benefit ends during the donor's lifetime, the gift is generally treated as a potentially exempt transfer or PET at that point, which is subject to inheritance tax on the donor's death where it occurs within seven years of the reservation ending.

The term 'gift' in the context of a GWR can include a sale deliberately made at undervalue.

The new legislation in Finance Act 1986 was designed to prevent taxpayers from 'having their cake and eating it' as it were. Without the GWR rules, an individual could make a potentially exempt gift of an asset but continue to have the use and enjoyment of it and after seven years, the property would be exempt from inheritance tax. The classic circumstances would have been for an individual to give away their home but to continue living in it. By the spring of 1986 that was no longer possible, but it didn't stop home-made planning based on the assumption that it was.

Inheritance tax planning schemes quickly evolved to circumvent the GWR rules. This resulted in an extension of the

GWR provisions in Finance Act 1999, dealing with arrangements involving interests in land and effective for disposals made on or after 9 March 1999. However, much inheritance tax planning continued to revolve around the donor gifting assets but continuing to benefit from them. The government finally introduced as a deterrent, in Finance Act 2004, an income tax charge on 'pre-owned assets' (often referred to as POAT). This income tax charge was introduced in response to certain inheritance tax planning arrangements with effect from the 2005/2006 tax year, although it applies with retroactive effect from 18 March 1986. Broadly speaking, an income tax liability may arise where a person occupies land that he has disposed of or has contributed (directly or indirectly) part of the consideration given by another person for the acquisition of the land.

But why is this of any relevance to investment property? Surely you either give a property away to a family member, it represents a PET and after seven years it is outside your estate or you give it to a trust as Alfred did and it is also out of your estate for inheritance tax purposes within seven years. If you do not survive the seven years it is deemed to be in your estate subject to tapering relief. Surely, POAT is not relevant? Alternatively, you don't give it away and it remains in your estate as with Aethelraed. In looking at the circumstances of Aethelraed and Alfred that is certainly correct.

However, there are circumstances where things are not quite so straightforward and consequently where opportunities lie in between the intersections of the anti-avoidance rules, the legislation, HMRC practice and the nature of what is given away. What if, say, you still received the rental income even though you have given the property away. By way of example chapter 9 looks at just one such possibility which shows that the innovative spirit we saw in the 1300's is still at work.

It depends on what you are giving away.

Here we are often looking at changing the nature of what is given away. Bear in mind that you don't need to be an expert in this. You will need to work with your accountant or solicitor and they should be able to do the heavy lifting for you. The object is of this book is to make you aware of what is possible. That is all. Most professionals considering something like a reversionary lease for the first time for instance will struggle with the technicalities. So, do not despair if you don't get it all at once.

Invariably, gifting debt or leaseholds or relying in changes in legislation are possibilities which may be of interest in your particular circumstances and that is what you can take away from the following chapters.

Use Mortgages

Instead of finding ingenious ways to transfer property to family members or trusts without incurring tax charges, you could instead consider taking out a mortgage secured on an existing property and then give away the cash. The gift would, of course, be a PET and so you would have to wait for the gift to fall outside your estate after seven years for it to be completely tax effective.

The value of the property in your estate is reduced by the mortgage for inheritance tax purposes which will be called in on your death but in the meantime you have essentially changed the nature of the gift from one of illiquid property into liquid cash which can be disposed of without capital gains tax implications.

More sophisticated variations of this strategy are the various debt schemes which some firms of accountants and solicitors offer to their clients. Just so that you can get a feel for what is out there I will briefly mention two of the most topical tactics.

The Family Debt Arrangement

Let us assume that one partner to a marriage, say the husband, owns a property. He could decide to sell the property to his wife at market value.

The wife does not have sufficient resources to acquire the property and so the consideration for the sale would be left outstanding as a debt to be repaid on the second death. The husband then assigns the debt to the couple's children or to a bare trust.

What are the tax implications?

There are no capital gains tax or pre-owned asset tax implications because of the inter-spouse transfer exemption for those taxes.

The property itself rests in the wife's estate following the transfer of legal and beneficial ownership but it is, of course, subject to the debt. The debt will reduce the value of the asset in the wife's estate.

The assignment of the debt is a PET but its value is discounted for inheritance tax purposes because of the repayment date.

There should be no gift with reservation implications where the debt is repayable on demand.

SDLT will be payable on the transfer since this is a sale.

The Family Partnership Debt Arrangement

Assume the same circumstances as above but the husband decides to transfer the property to a husband and wife partnership. The consideration is left outstanding as debt as before.

The husband & wife assign the debt to their children or a bare trust.

What are the tax Implications?

There is no capital gains tax event because there is no change in beneficial interest.

There are no pre-owned asset tax implications because the value remains in the couple's estate.

The assignment of the debt is, of course, a PET but it is also discounted because of the repayment date.

There should be no gift with reservation implications if debt is repayable on demand.

All these tactics rely on changing the nature of what is being gifted to get around the reality that the underlying value is represented by illiquid property which is also exposed to capital gains tax.

The safest of these strategies is undoubtedly the mortgage because the debt originates with an independent third party who will also naturally ensure that all the formalities and technicalities are assiduously complied with. It will also be secured against the property and a charge placed on it. Land Registry records will doubtless show that charge.

This is not the case with the two debt-based arrangements, and you would therefore require a professional such as an accountant or a solicitor to ensure that all the formalities and technicalities are in place. You may rest assured that HMRC will always distinguish between a plausible story (or what I call 'let's just say' tax planning) from what has actually transpired. Home-made execution will almost certainly be unpicked and unravelled by HMRC where things do not stack up.

Chapter 8 – Sophisticated Planning: The Reversionary Lease

Continuing the theme of changing the nature of what is given away, why not create a leasehold interest, retain the freehold and give away the leasehold? How would this work?

The owner of a freehold investment property grants a long lease with a term of, say, 195 years but which does not give the lessee possession of the property until some future date. A reversionary lease is simply a lease with a deferred start date. As the lease does not create any rights immediately it may be called a deferred or reversionary lease.

The maximum period during which the lessee's right to possession may be postponed is 21 years. The terms of the lease would be expressed to confer possession on whichever is the first to occur of the 21st anniversary of the lease or the donor's death. The donee, the recipient, is likely to be an individual or the trustees of a settlement. Until the 21st anniversary of the lease the donor continues to receive the rental income from the property by virtue of the retention of the freehold. On the 21st anniversary the donor would lose the right to receive rent.

The freehold continues to have a value in the donor's hands, but that value will depend upon actuarial calculations, since the reversionary lease would be expressed to come into possession on the death of the donor if that occurs before the 21st anniversary. The retained interest in the freehold may possibly be worth around 40%-50% of the original unencumbered freehold, but that would depend on circumstances and professional valuations.

The grant of the lease immediately reduces the value of the freehold by that proportion initially and then the value continues to decrease in value each year as the day of the leasehold approaches. If the donor survives until the 21st anniversary of the lease, the freehold reversion to the lease would at that stage have a negligible value, let us say 5% for illustrative purposes.

The value of the freehold, subject to the lease, remains in the donor's estate for inheritance tax purposes. Just as in the 1300's, a lot of the value appears to have disappeared for tax purposes because it rests in the lease

The Income Tax Effects?

The donor continues to receive rent by virtue of retaining the freehold interest until the reversionary lease takes effect.

There are no POAT implications since while there is a disposal of an interest in land there is no occupation – Finance Act 2004 Schedule 15 para 3(1)(a). The property is an investment property.

The Inheritance Tax Effects?

The gift of the lease represents a PET if made to an individual or a chargeable lifetime transfer if to a trust. In the case of a gift to a trust the intention would be that the value of the lease at the time of the gift would be within the nil rate band and therefore that there is no charge to inheritance tax.

The retained freehold diminishes in value over time, reducing the value of the estate until the start date of the lease commences by which time the almost the full value of the property will have transferred to the donee.

It is considered that in principle reversionary leases are not caught by the gift with reservation provisions because the basic conditions must be satisfied for there to be a reservation of benefit:

Firstly, the taxpayer disposes of an interest in land by way of gift. This the donor undoubtedly does when he or she grants the beneficiary the deferred lease - Finance Act 1986 s 102A(1).

Secondly, he or she must retain "a significant right or interest or (be) party to a significant arrangement in relation to the land."

Does retaining the freehold interest satisfy the second requirement? It all depends on the facts and circumstances since "a right or interest is not significant if it was granted or acquired before the period of seven years ending with the date of the gift." – Finance Act 1986 s 102A(5).

If one were implementing this type of planning then one would undoubtedly ensure that the property had been owned for well over seven years and the freehold itself had been acquired. It may therefore be considered that the let out applies and so the gifted lease is not property subject to a reservation; depending on individual circumstances and the manner in which it is implemented.

This also appears to be the stated view of HM Revenue & Customs in their Inheritance Tax Manual paragraph 14360 where the freehold interest was acquired more than seven years before the gift provided the lease contains no benefits or covenants. The terms on which the reversionary lease is granted would, no doubt, not entail the payment of rent or impose any covenants mirroring those in any headlease (and so the case of Buzzoni, for instance, would not be relevant ... but that is another story).

The Capital Gains Tax Effects?

Complex but manageable.

On Grant of the Lease

If no premium is paid on the grant of a lease, no chargeable gain will accrue but this is only provided that the grant of the lease was an arm's length transaction. Whether the gift is to individuals or to a trust that will be a difficult position to maintain.

It is therefore thought that Taxation of Chargeable Gains Act 1992 section 17 (disposals and acquisitions deemed to occur at market value) will operate since the lease is granted between connected persons or is otherwise granted not at arm's length. The tenant is consequently deemed to have acquired the lease at its market value and have paid the appropriate premium.

Additionally, an imputed premium which is deemed to arise in these circumstances is to be treated for capital gains tax purposes in precisely the same way as any other premium.

This is confirmed by HM Revenue & Customs in their capital Gains Tax Manual paragraph 70825.

The grant of the reversionary lease (which is a long lease) at the outset would represent a part disposal for capital gains tax purposes.

The capital gain on grant would be based on the value of the imputed premium for the deemed disposal proceeds. The allowable cost to set against that imputed premium would be represented by the cost of the freehold as adjusted using the A/A+B part disposal formulae found in the Taxation of Chargeable Gains Act 1992 section 42 where A is the value of imputed premium and B is the value of the freehold reversion. It is therefore essential to obtain independent and sustainable valuations for the imputed premium and for the freehold reversion in the particular circumstances under consideration.

If the lease were granted to a relevant property trust the gain arising could be held over, of course.

On a Future Sale

The recipient(s) of the lease would have a low capital gains tax base value for their interest in the property. The determination of the value of the reversionary lease would be guided by actuarial factors. This could be, say, 50% - 60% of the original unencumbered freehold value. The potential capital gains tax on a future sale could potentially represent a problem for the donee.

However, this downside would equally have existed had nothing at all been done and, in any event, is subject to two interesting caveats:

Firstly, no doubt the owner of the reversionary lease would seek to acquire the donor's freehold reversion from the donor's executors after his or her death to reunite all the interests in one pair of hands.

Secondly, this type of planning favours the long-term property investor and if there is unlikely to be any intention to sell the property at a future point the capital gains tax implications are unlikely to be a practical issue.

It has to be accepted that there will be no worthwhile uplift in the capital gains tax base cost on the donors death but that should be balanced against the considerable inheritance tax savings coupled with the reality that the property is likely to remain within the wider family rather than being sold in the medium to longer term.

SDLT Implications

The transfer of the lease to the donee represents a gift so there is no SDLT liability - Finance Act 2003, Schedule 3 paragraph 1.

Could Alfred have used this?

Alfred could have considered using a reversionary lease to transfer his property. Let us assume that Alfred had three properties. The current value of the three properties is £900,000. Alfred could not afford to give all three properties away as he would lose the rental income and, in an ideal world, would like to keep the rent for 15 years but give away the capital value. He therefore grants a reversionary lease (vesting after 15 years) to a settlement for his adult children. He retains the rent because he remains the freeholder. The property's value on the transfer to the trust is heavily depleted because of the deferral. The value settled in these circumstances is unlikely to me more than £325,000.

Because Alfred has used a trust, capital gains tax holdover relief is available to cover the imputed premium.

By virtue of Finance Act 1986 section 102A(5) there is no gift with reservation of benefit given that Alfred has owned the property for more than seven years.

If the property subject to the reversionary lease is occupied by the disponer, there will be a potential pre-owned asset charge. However, where the property is rented out there is no charge because it is Alfred's tenant, not Alfred, who is occupying the property.

Alfred should also consider that such planning might ultimately fall within DOTAS.

Bear in mind that all we have been describing is a possibility and running through some of the tax implications. Those implications must be embedded in the implementation, proper professional valuations and analysis as well as a commercial rationale for the planning.

Hard? You bet it is and so it should be.

It was harder in the 1300's!

Nevertheless, a professional adviser will be able to do the heavy lifting for you provided you know what you are trying to achieve.

Chapter 9 - Sophisticated Planning: The Income Property Trust

Where you are about to acquire a property or you have only recently acquired it, it is well worth considering the use of a property income trust. This will allow you to retain the income arising from the property while placing the property outside of your estate for inheritance tax purposes.

Instead of giving property to an individual for inheritance tax planning purposes you could consider transferring it to a life interest relevant property trust. That is, a formal trust in which the beneficiary has an interest in possession and so is entitled by right to income as it arises.

The transfer to the trust represents a chargeable lifetime transfer and therefore the value of the property transferred should be under the available inheritance tax nil rate band. The property is outside your estate after seven years. While the life tenant receives and is taxed on rental income, there is no GWR.

Astonishing?

The Background

Since 1986 it has been possible to make what are known as potentially exempt transfers – gifts that fall within the so-called "seven-year rule". Broadly speaking, most outright gifts by one individual to another (and until March 2006 most gifts into trust) are only liable to inheritance tax if the person making the gift dies within the seven years following the gift.

After this rule came in there was a demand from people who wanted to make a gift which was effective for inheritance tax purposes, but which still gave them access to the property which they had given away. The inheritance tax rules have been progressively tightened over the years to combat various schemes and planning ideas along these lines. As a result, the vast majority of inheritance tax arrangements which are designed to enable you to "have your cake and eat it" will either be treated as gifts with reservation or will be liable to pre-owned assets income tax. These rules have already been considered in Chapter 7.

If a gift is treated as a "gift with reservation" then for inheritance tax purposes the gifted property is still deemed to be within the donor's estate. In those cases where the donor has reserved a benefit in such a way that the gift with reservation rules do not apply, then there is a strong likelihood that the donor will be liable to pay income tax at his marginal rate on the assessed value of the interest which he has retained in the gifted property.

In this case, the case of the income property trust, the settlor has not retained any interest in the capital, and therefore the settlement is not caught by the gift with reservation of benefit provisions of Finance Act 1986 Schedule 20.

The Opportunity Provided by Finance Act 2006

Finance Act 2006 enacted substantial changes to the inheritance tax treatment of trusts. In particular, most interest in possession trusts are now subject to the same inheritance tax rules as discretionary trusts. In the past, for inheritance tax purposes, the person who was entitled to the income from the life interest trust was deemed to own the capital. This is no longer the case. Accordingly, it is possible to take advantage of the fact that in the future one can use a trust to separate the ownership of the underlying capital from the entitlement to the income of the trust.

The Planning

Alfred creates a life interest trust. The terms of the trust are that Alfred is entitled to the income of the trust for the rest of his lifetime. Thereafter the trust capital passes to Alfred's chosen beneficiaries as set down in the trust deed. The trust deed will strictly prohibit Alfred from ever receiving any of the capital of the trust.

The Inheritance Tax Analysis of the Trust

Although Alfred has retained the right to receive the trust income, he has given away the trust capital. He no longer has any access to it. Once Alfred has survived for seven years after making the gift into trust, the value of the gift is not liable to inheritance tax on the occasion of his death. Any increase in the value of the trust fund is not liable to inheritance tax on Alfred's death in any event.

The gift into trust is a chargeable transfer for inheritance tax purposes. As long as Alfred does not make a gift into trust which takes his seven year history of chargeable transfers above the inheritance tax threshold (currently £325,000) the gift into trust will not be liable to inheritance tax. If the gift exceeds the inheritance tax threshold then the excess will be immediately liable to inheritance tax at 20%. In short, Alfred can give away some of his capital but retain the right to income from the capital for the rest of his lifetime.

The Limitations on Investing the Trust Fund

In order to avoid liability to pre-owned assets income tax, the trust fund may only invest in land or buildings not occupied by Alfred. The property is let out to tenants and is therefore residential property. As the property is let it is therefore not occupied. The POAT rules do not extend to immoveable property that is not occupied by the GWR provisions. Finance Act 2004.Paragraph 3(1)(a) of Schedule 15.

Therefore, the following types of investment would be permissible:

- buy to let property;
- commercial or industrial property;
- a house or flat for occupation by Alfred's children or grandchildren while they are at university;
- land which is being retained because it may have development potential in the future.

Buy to Let and Trustee Borrowings

If Alfred's objective is to maximise the inheritance tax planning opportunities, he will want to contribute the maximum amount of cash to the trust, e.g. £325,000.

Clients of more modest means may wish to put a smaller amount of cash into the trust but then for the trustees to borrow additional funds to enable them to acquire a more expensive property. Although the initial gift will be for a smaller amount, the value of the trust fund outside of Alfred's estate will increase both as a result of capital appreciation on the buy to let property and also as the borrowings are repaid.

If Alfred is active in the buy to let market he may therefore be interested in structuring some of his future acquisitions through a trust on the basis that, as long as the buy to let can provide him with a measure of income, he is happy for the capital and future growth in property values to be outside of his estate for the benefit of his children and grandchildren.

Transferring an Existing Property

Any existing property owned by Alfred but which is not going to be occupied by him in the future could be transferred to the trust. However, the transfer to the trustees will trigger a deemed disposal for capital gains tax purposes and capital gains tax may therefore be payable. Payment of the tax cannot be deferred. Why?

The downside of this type of trust is that of capital gains tax on the transfer to it. The income property trust is clearly a settlor interested trust and therefore it is not possible to holdover any gains because of the anti-avoidance rule in the Taxation of Chargeable Gains Act 992 sections 169B – 169C. For this reason, the trust is really only suitable where you have a new property which has not had the opportunity to build up any chargeable gains or where the gift into trust is initially of cash and the property will be acquired by the trustees at a later date.

The Potential Attitude of HM Revenue & Customs

The planning outlined flows as a natural consequence of the changes to the rules for life interest trusts introduced in the Finance Act 2006.

The arrangement has many similarities to insurance based discounted gift schemes which have been around for many years and have successfully survived recent crackdowns on inheritance tax planning.

The planning is, however, both simpler and more transparent than a discounted gift scheme. It also permits Alfred, if he is one of the trustees, to be fully in control of the investment process.

The idea represents a subtle play on the legislation but with a considerable tax advantage.

Part IV - What About a Company?

Chapter 10 – A Company?

Alfred was successful in firing up the enthusiasm of his children, Edward and Aethelflaed for investment property. As a result of Alfred's planning, his property portfolio remained largely intact and, under his guidance, his children had some years of property management experience under their belt by the time he died. His son and daughter had a 50% share, in trust, in each property they acquired in Alfred's lifetime. As they grew older and wiser the trustees passed the properties to them absolutely and, once again, holdover relief ensured that no capital gains tax was payable on the transfer.

Over the next few years the business prospered, and a dozen properties were acquired. As the families of Edward and Aethelflaed grew the siblings began to reflect on a better way to run their full-time business. It was becoming unwieldy and they felt that the solution to the greater complexity they were encountering could lie in a company.

But how is it that they came to consider a vehicle which was other than the trusts which had served the family well?

Their problem was that although trusts remain useful, we have seen that it is no longer possible (since 2006) to transfer unlimited amounts into a lifetime trust without triggering an immediate inheritance tax charge. Since March 2006 an immediate inheritance tax charge at 20% is levied on assets transferred into any relevant property trust to the extent that the gift into trust exceeds the donor's unused nil rate band. The current nil rate band is £325,000.

What they really wanted to do is stay in the game and expand their property empire, not step back from it, but they realised that this strategy brought huge risks when it came to their estates and the impact of inheritance tax. To address both issues, expansion and tax, meant that they would be forced to take succession planning and family involvement as seriously as their father had done and take responsibility for driving things forward.

Traditionally, trusts have been used to enable assets to pass down a generation for inheritance tax purposes without giving control of the assets to younger family members. The younger members of the family would be beneficiaries of the trust, but the trust assets would be controlled by the trustees, who would typically be senior family members.

A company, by contrast, represents a structure which facilitates the making of gifts which do not trigger any immediate liability to inheritance tax at 20% on amounts over £325,000 (i.e. the current nil rate band where unused). The problem lies in ensuring that the younger generation will find it difficult to obtain access to liquid assets without the agreement of the senior members of the family ... as we have seen with Alfred.

A trust offers a well-established route of achieving this but is it possible for a company structure to achieve the same outcome? That depends entirely on how things are structured.

Before looking in a little more detail at some of the planning ideas which are open to Edward and Aethelflaed, we need to consider precisely the nature of the company which they are looking at. For most, a company is a company but when it comes to property investment companies that is an oversimplification. Tread the usual path and efforts are likely to become unfocussed.

Chapter 11 - The Family Investment Company

A word on the family investment company before continuing. Family investment companies were first designed for estate planning following the massive changes to the taxation of trusts in 2006. The idea was to take a company and make it mirror many of the advantages of a flexible discretionary trust but without the same tax treatment. Of course, a company is never as flexible as a trust, but it does provide a structure that separates ownership from control ... which is also a key feature of a trust and of most estate and inheritance tax planning. This characteristic enables families to pass wealth down the generations without giving up control of how the wealth is invested and when benefits are received by the next generation.

The potential inheritance tax benefit of the company comes from three key sources.

The first is the reduction in the value of the estate for the founders of the family investment company. They will generally make a gift on the formation of the company, by either passing some shares or cash for the subscription of shares to children/grandchildren. Sometimes cash is also gifted to a family trust, which will then subscribe for shares. These initial gifts save inheritance tax completely if the donor then survives seven years. There is no limit on such gifts unlike for trusts.

The second benefit comes from the way shares are valued. If a family member has a minority interest in the company, their shares are likely to attract a discount to reflect the size of interest. Discounts for investment companies are not the same as for trading companies but can still be advantageous. The cumulative effect of the discounts when looking at a family as a whole, can add up to significant valuation reductions and that value is not then subject to inheritance tax.

The final benefit is that a family investment company is not within the relevant property regime and so is not subject to ten-year anniversary charges of up to 6% or exit charges as would be the case for a new trust.

Family investment companies can also offer protection from the impact of a divorce in the family and this advantage is considered further below and in appendix IV.

When family investment companies were first being incorporated as an estate planning tool post 2006, their corporation tax treatment was not particularly favourable. The corporation tax rate has since been reduced and currently stands at 19% which looks attractive compared to a trust paying 45% on its income. However, there is another layer of tax that must be paid when profits are distributed to shareholders and the cumulative effect of the two layers of tax mean that a family investment company is not particularly tax efficient if the intention is for all profits to be distributed annually. However, where profits are intended to be accumulated to grow the family wealth, then a family investment company can start to become very tax efficient.

A cautionary note when it comes to income tax planning with such companies.

Low rates of corporation tax have led to an increase in the use of companies to hold investments. Such companies are sometimes referred to as personal investment companies or PIC's. Their structure tends to be much more straightforward and is generally funded mainly by debt. The aim of the structure is to enable capital to be invested by the company, accumulating profits in the more favourable corporate tax regime. Capital is easily extracted in the form of loan repayments. Profits are also extracted by way of dividends which are taxable, but the timing and the level of dividends can be controlled to minimise tax liabilities. The main purpose of this type of company is to control and minimise income tax.

An advantage of the personal investment company is that it would be easy to wind up if the corporation tax rules change to make the structure less attractive. Winding up does of course have tax implications of its own that would have to be considered but if no other shareholders are involved and the share capital is straightforward the process will be much easier than for a family investment company.

A family investment company is likely to be more complicated as share ownership is much wider and may include minors and other individuals that you do not wish to distribute large capital sums to.

When most people approach their accountant to set up a property company what they are often engaged in is income tax mitigation. They are running a personal investment company rather than a family investment company. A completely different type of animal with a different outcome to the family investment company.

Hybrid Planning & A Warning

The aims of a family investment company are very different to a personal investment company because a family investment company is designed as a vehicle to hold investments for the family while protecting and controlling the capital. Given the different objectives, attempting to build a single company to achieve both aims can lead to complexity and potentially increased risk of anti-avoidance rules applying.

When referring to companies in this book, we are talking about the family investment company. For many readers, it may be useful to know something about investment companies even if they are already decided or will decide in the future, not to adopt that route. For those who wish to explore family investment companies in a little more depth, appendices II, III and IV draw attention to some of the absolutely essential considerations with respect to capital structure, control and asset protection respectively while appendices V, VI and VII look at potential funding issues, anti-avoidance legislation and the settlements legislation respectively.

The appendices are there to illustrate precisely how you structure your share capital, how you control and manage your company and how you take steps to protect the company assets from all manner of calamities. That can have a decisive effect on the family assets and your inheritance tax position. A good accountant or solicitor can assist with the technicalities but it is important that you understand your circumstances and your direction of travel. As well as nailing your circumstances to the ground from the outset it is essential in informing you of what you are striving to achieve and how the above issues are dealt with....or not.

With respect to the two appendices on anti-avoidance legislation, while it is important to be aware of it, it is for your professional adviser to dovetail planning with this in mind. The 'transactions in securities' and 'settlements legislation' are really sending a message to taxpayers. That message is not be too clever for your own good. An arrangement may be 'super convenient' but you may just be offering HMRC the best opportunity you can for them to unpick a structure. Skim read the anti-avoidance appendices and use them for reference by all means but don't dwell on them too much.

Even if you are not considering a company in the foreseeable future it makes sense to be familiar with the planning ideas as who can say what you will need in the next five to ten years or when new properties are acquired.

In my experience when most people have a company owning investment property what they actually have is a personal investment company. It is easily identified by asking three questions:

- Show me the articles of association – They are usually of the 'off the shelf' variety.
- Show me the shareholders agreement – There isn't a shareholder's agreement.
- Show me the capital structure of the company – Just ordinary shares.

Those responses look like a fairly obvious personal investment company!

Nevertheless, even a simple company of this type can yield impressive results in the right hands. Consider the skeletal facts of a real-life example.

Instead of holding an investment property 100% personally, a taxpayer arranged the acquisition of a new and valuable property to be through a new company. The shareholders were husband 25%, wife 25%, adult son 25% and adult daughter-in-law 25%. On the wife's death, her 25% share was agreed with HMRC as subject to a 40% discount so that the value in her estate amounted to 15% of the property value (i.e. 60% x 25%). Her 25% share passed to the children and was covered by her nil rate band for inheritance tax purposes. When her husband dies, instead of suffering inheritance tax on 100% of the property value, he will at worst have a 15% share in his estate. In practice it will be less than this.

Brilliant but simple planning from someone with vision! Planning does not have to be as complex as that set out in in Chapters 8 and 9.

Chapter 12 - Planning in Practice

Back to Edward and Aethelflaed.

Assume that Edward and Aethelflaed wish to start the process of passing wealth to their children and grandchildren. Initially they were thinking in terms of using a company for new acquisitions. Edward and Aethelflaed would establish the company and invest £1million in cash in return for shares. They might then give some of those shares to their children. If they did so the value in the shares would constitute a PET. They might also decide to establish a discretionary trust for their grandchildren and gift shares in the company to the discretionary trust. If they did so this would be immediately chargeable to inheritance tax but assuming that they have not made any previous chargeable transfers in the last seven years, Edward and Aethelflaed could each gift shares up to £325,000 in value to the discretionary trust without suffering a tax charge as we saw in chapter 6. They could also establish bare trusts for the benefit of their existing grandchildren who are currently under 18. A gift to a bare trust does not result in any immediate liability to inheritance tax. It is a PET.

None of these transactions would suffer a capital gains tax charge because there is no gain at this point.

At a later date Edward and Aethelflaed might choose to gift further shares to the children or grandchildren. If the shares had risen in value then capital gains tax would be a consideration, but that would be the case whether one was talking about shares in a company or any other asset that has risen in value other than cash.

As with any company, control will be in the hands of the company's board of directors. When the company is set up, restrictions can be included in the company's constitution which will effectively allow Edward and Aethelflaed to remain as directors and control the company for as long as they wish. The articles of association can be drafted to ensure that only suitable senior members of the family may be appointed as directors. The articles of association of the company are a public document, filed at Companies House. It may be appropriate to supplement the articles of association with a shareholders' agreement, which is not a public document. The shareholders' agreement might regulate the powers of the directors. This would be particularly important if the founder of the company does not wish to be a director. The shareholders' agreement could provide that certain key decisions affecting the company require the consent of the founder. The shareholders' agreement might also place limits on the persons that may hold shares in the company.

One of the concerns when considering lifetime giving is the worry that children or grandchildren might behave irresponsibly with any valuable asset which they receive. If you give a child cash or a portfolio of quoted shares, they might be tempted to spend the money unwisely. On the other hand, shares in an unquoted family company are likely to be wholly unmarketable by their very nature.

There is no reason why the company's constitution cannot also provide that shares may only be transferred to descendants of Edward and Aethelflaed. That effectively prevents any of the children converting their shareholding into cash without the agreement of Edward and Aethelflaed. The husband or wife of a child or grandchild would probably not be permitted to hold shares in the company.

What happens if Edward and Aethelflaed decide to treat their three children equally but are worried about giving assets to one in particular because they don't care for his or her spouse? Giving the adult child shares in the company is likely to be significantly safer than giving cash or property assets. The divorce courts will normally have the ability to vary the terms of a trust. However, the courts cannot normally "pierce the corporate veil" and will not be able to interfere in the affairs of the company. If the adult child were to get divorced, then the value of his or her shares in the company will be taken account of when computing the extent of their true wealth. Even here, the child will only have a small minority shareholding and the shares should attract a substantial discount as compared to the net asset value of the company. Valuation of shares subject to restrictions would be a priority.

Currently, a company will normally pay corporation tax at 19% on its income and gains.

Shareholders should always be aware that potentially there is a double tax charge because shareholders may have further tax to pay on dividend income from the company (currently 7.5% at the basic rate, 32.5% at the higher rate and 38.1% at the additional rate, subject to the dividend allowance) and will pay capital gains tax on any gains arising if they sell or gift their shares. That is one reason why it might be particularly useful for the founder's grandchildren to be issued with a different class of share. Where the shareholders are higher rate taxpayers it will usually be appropriate to retain income within the company so that it can benefit from the lower rates of tax payable by the company. In addition, dividend income received by the company from another UK company will not suffer any further corporation tax from the company. This is particularly favourable when compared with a discretionary trust.

It is the case that the company will pay corporation tax on its chargeable gains and that if shareholders dispose of shares or the company is wound up then capital gains tax becomes payable on the gains made by the shareholders as well. However, if it is intended that the company should remain in existence in the longer term with shares passing down through the family, capital gains tax on the sale of shares is unlikely to be a major issue.

Two points to reflect on.

Firstly, a sale of shares or a gift of shares between family members would be chargeable to capital gains tax on the difference between market value at the time of transfer and the base cost of the shares on general principles.

Secondly, a transfer of assets from the company to family members would almost certainly be charged to income tax as a distribution, remuneration or a benefit.

In this sense, incorporation would seem to be fairly neutral which achieves little. The attraction, however, lies in the increased flexibility a company offers for planning.

There are a few possibilities which are worthy of attention if the properties were to be held through a company.

What if you have several properties or your portfolio runs into millions? A property company will save you tax as the rents are taxable at 19% rather than at the directors' highest marginal rate. But what if the property is not already in the company? You have a capital gains tax problem.

Years down the line Alfred's son and daughter have more properties and they are the first generation of the family which has learnt the importance of family and has developed idea's which inherited from their father.

Chapter 13 - Discounted Share Values

A major reason why the use of a company can be particularly tax efficient is that the total value of all the various shareholdings can be significantly less than the full value of the company on an asset basis. That will be of clear interest with respect to the capital taxes.

It is common for the articles of association of private companies to place restrictions on the transfer of shares to protect the founders of the company, or a controlling group, from the dangers of shares passing into the hands of unwelcome shareholders as we have seen earlier. The effect of these restrictions, combined with various company law rules on when the shareholders of the company may pass ordinary or special resolutions, means that small minority shareholdings, say 25% or less, are often valued at a substantial discount to full asset value. The discount will ultimately be a matter for expert negotiation with HM Revenue & Customs Shares and Assets Valuation Section, but it could be as much as between 50% and 75%. Holdings between 26% and 50% of total share capital will benefit from a lower discount which may be between 25% and 50%.

Incorporation can then, in principle, offer two immediate inheritance tax planning advantages. For illustrative purposes let us assume a property investment company with a value of £3 million and a capital gains tax base cost of £1 million. In other words, the company is sitting on capital gains of £2 million.

Firstly, there would be an immediate reduction for inheritance tax purposes in the value of the property represented by the shares. A 25% discount for, say, a 46% holding would amount to an inheritance tax saving of £138,000 and a 50% discount £276,000, for instance.

Secondly, a discounted valuation for capital gains tax purposes would enable shareholdings to be passed around the family more effectively simply because the value and therefore the capital gain is lower. Transfers of shares around the family will still potentially incur capital gains tax liabilities. It is just that the values involved may be somewhat lower because of the discount.

If one gifted a property worth £3 million to an individual on this basis it would take 167 years to make the transfer in tranches using the annual exemption to cover the capital gain. If there were two of you it would take 84 years. Impractical even ignoring the inevitable growth in property values. You would have to start planning long before you were born!

To do the same but gifting to a trust with no limit on the gain which could be held over but with a limit of the nil rate band

Inheritance Tax Planning   Steve Parnham

threshold every seven years it would take 65 years to pass it into trust or 33 years if there were two of you (i.e. a married couple or civil partners). Still a long time ... but more manageable.

Using a company however and assuming a 25% discount and a discounted capital gain, it would take 125 years to pass to an individual and 63 if there were two of you.

If the shares went to a trust the same process would take 49 years or 25 years if there were two of you.

It is still a long time but less than currently exists where transfers between individuals are involved. Transferring property to individuals without trusts cannot be done tax free where gains are significant. Using trusts and companies can speed things up. Even in this example with its huge capital gain, it would be possible to move much quicker using the techniques in Chapters 14 and 15 in conjunction with discounted share values and, of course, it is also wise to remember that it is never all or nothing when it comes to inheritance tax. A more modest gifting strategy over 10 or 20 years will still have a very significant impact on the inheritance tax payable at the end of the day. If the shareholdings can be fragmented around members of the family or family trusts over time, it is quite possible for the shares to benefit from substantial discounts on asset value for tax purposes so that much of the value in the company then escapes the capital taxes system entirely. Of course, achieving this fragmentation can itself incur tax charges.

This will not eliminate the inheritance tax by any means, but it will make a significant dent in the potential liability through discounts and through assisting a gifting strategy.

Incidentally, the above examples are purely for illustrative purposes. It is quite difficult to make direct comparisons between the individual, trust and corporate positions because of the assumptions on which these comparisons are inevitably based. For comparative purposes the corporate examples assume that one individual (or two where one considers a spouse or civil partner) owns all the shares and yet obtains a 25% discount for lack of marketability. In practice that is unlikely. In practice the individual will be looking at a less than 75% or even less than 50% shareholding because of the spread of ownership throughout the family and therefore a considerably reduced exposure to inheritance tax. The point of the comparison, however, is to point to the passage of time which is required to pass value without triggering a capital gains tax charge.

This discounted minority value principle is subject to a rule which aggregates all shares given to 'connected persons' within a six-year period by any one individual.

A word of caution. Valuing a shareholding is by no means straightforward. It could, for instance, be argued that a 46% interest in the company may constitute a controlling holding. How so?

'Controlling interest' is a situation where one person or entity holds more than half of the voting shares. In general, it places the single person or entity in a position where, even if all other shareholders vote in opposition to a decision supported by the investor with a majority of voting shares, their collective strength will not be sufficient to alter the decision. In most cases, this situation is present when a single investor owns in excess of half of the shares currently in circulation, although in other instances, it may require something more.

For instance, and depending on the articles of incorporation of a given company, a two-thirds majority vote of shareholders may be required in order to approve a decision. If that is the case, an investor who owned just over half of the outstanding shares would not be able to control the outcome alone. He or she would still require the support of at least enough of the other investors to achieve two thirds vote in favour of the issue.

In another sense, a controlling interest may also be present when a single investor owns at least 34% of the voting stock currently in circulation. This might be the case when a two-thirds majority vote is required to approve an issue that is put before the shareholders. Without winning the support of the single investor who controls 34% of the shares, there is no way to achieve that majority and the issue will be defeated. From this perspective, an investor can be considered both a minority investor and still have control, in that nothing is likely to pass without his or her support.

Nevertheless, the principle is clear.

Chapter 14 - Different Share Classes

The structure of a company can be kept very simple by just having the one class of ordinary shares as is typical with a personal investment company.

It is possible, however, to have different classes of shares. If all of Edward and Aethelflaed's children had a different class of ordinary share it would be possible for the directors in this way to provide income to a particular shareholder just by declaring a dividend in respect of the class of shares held by that particular individual. If multiple share classes are to be used, then ideally this should be introduced when the company is established. Creation of different share classes later will raise tax issues which will require careful consideration.

Shares may be classified as ordinary, preference and redeemable and can have a mixture of income and capital rights depending on family needs. They may also be voting or non-voting shares. The combinations are almost limitless but will always be driven by having a well thought through analysis of where the family is with respect to estate planning and where it intends to be over the next 10- 20 years as a minimum.

These issues are set out in a more detail in appendix II and will invariably entail bespoke articles of association rather than the 'off the shelf' variety.

Chapter 15 – Freezing Growth

Earlier, in chapter 4, Alfred was very focussed on the problem of the future growth in his property. Commercially, of course, that is hardly a problem but in terms of inheritance tax it clearly is one. Given that shares in property investment companies never qualify for business reliefs (subject to the possibility set out in Chapter 17) other alternatives need to be sought out to minimise inheritance tax liabilities. 'Freezing' is a method of dealing with that problem of growth.

Where the capital gains tax liability on a gift of shares is too large to be acceptable, with or without discounts, or where significant growth in asset values can be anticipated, one might consider freezing the value of the company shares to tackle the issue.

Typically, this will involve pegging the value of the owner's property company shares and passing any future growth to the next generation.

The first step is to create a new class of growth share, usually by way of a bonus issue. These new shares will only be entitled to dividends and participation in any winding up proceeds once the present value of the company has been distributed to the holders of the original shares. The rights attaching to these original shares are altered to restrict their future dividends and winding up proceeds to an aggregate sum equal to the current value of the company. This will have the immediate effect of freezing their value at that amount.

The new shares will be initially worth very little but hopefully they will grow significantly in value in line with property prices over the coming years. It is these new shares which are given to the donor's children or to a trust for their benefit.

This involves issuing new B share capital which effectively freezes the value of the existing ordinary shares. The new B shares will have no dividend rights to current profits but they will have contingent rights to future enhanced profits. Rights to assets on a winding up will be similarly divided. Provided that this mechanism is properly set up and implemented, it should be possible to give away the new B shares free of any capital gains tax liability.

The new growth shares initially should be worth very little, and might possibly have nil value, but may grow significantly in value in the coming years. The new shares could be given to adult children, but where the future growth may be substantial, a trust (or trusts) may be a more suitable recipient.

These B shares are only entitled to dividends and entitlements on winding up once the current value of the company has been distributed to the holders of the existing class of shares.

The rights attaching to the existing shares are altered to restrict their dividends and entitlements on winding-up to a total amount equal to the current value of the company and so freeze their value. This is invariably best demonstrated by way of example.

An Example: Alfred's Grandson

Athelstan holds 100% of a UK company that in turn holds various residential investment properties. The value of the company is currently £2 million.

A new class of 'B' shares is issued to him. The articles of association of the company are amended so that the 'B' shares are entitled to dividends and capital on winding up only to the extent that the existing 'A' shares have received £2 million by way of dividend or capital. The 'B' shares are initially worthless or worth very little.

Athelstan makes a gift of the 'B' shares to a discretionary trust for his adult children and future generations.

Athelstan dies ten years later when the company is worth £4 million. The 'A' shares have paid total dividends of £750,000 over the five years. Therefore the 'A' shares are then worth £1.25 million, and the 'B' shares are worth £2.75 million.

The 'B' shares have captured the future growth of £2.75 million and the 'A' shares have been frozen at £2 million (less dividends received).

The inheritance tax saving is 40% of the £2.75 million, being £1.1million. A massive tax saving!

The Capital Gains Tax Analysis?

The bonus issue of new shares and reorganisation of the original share capital will fall within the reconstruction rules, with the result that there is no disposal for capital gains tax purposes on issue – Taxation of Chargeable Gains Act 1992 section 127.

The gift of the B shares to the trust represents a disposal at market value. However, the deemed proceeds are nil or, more likely, very small since very little growth will have occurred provided that the settlor, the settlor's spouse and minor children are excluded from benefit.

If the shares are transferred into trust, capital gains tax holdover relief will be available in any event provided the settlor, spouse, civil partner and minor children of the settlor are excluded from benefit.

The Inheritance Tax Analysis?

The reconstruction itself will not be a chargeable event for inheritance tax purposes, but the gift of shares will be a potentially exempt transfer, if made to the children, or a chargeable lifetime transfer, if made to most types of trust.

If a full nil rate band is available, then as long as it is clear that the value is well within the nil rate band a detailed valuation negotiation with HMRC shares valuation may not be required.

If you have made potentially exempt transfers, and you were to die within seven years, these will become chargeable transfers and may exhaust the nil rate band, which will impact on the inheritance tax position of the new trust. It may be appropriate to consider short-term life insurance cover depending on the specific circumstances.

Valuations?

It is recommended to involve a share valuation specialist both to value the company and confirm the initial low or nil value of the growth shares. Sometimes it is wise to err on the side of caution. For example, if it is thought that the company is worth £2 million, perhaps set the freezer hurdle at £2.5 million?

It should be understood by the existing owner that future dividend entitlement from the retained shares is capped under this arrangement. Where the owner has received substantial dividends from their property investment company over the years, how comfortable do they feel about the source of their income drying up at some stage in the future?

Chapter 16 - Incorporation of an Investment Property Portfolio?

Earlier Edward and Aethelfraed were considering setting up a company for all new property purchases. As cash was injected there were no capital gains tax issues to struggle with.

But is it possible to incorporate an existing property business without suffering capital gains tax? The simple answer is 'Yes' in principle but very much depending on the circumstances.

Edward and Aethelfraed could equally have decided to transfer their existing dozen or so properties into a company for the benefits we have already discussed. The potential problem with this approach is that it can easily give rise to a substantial capital gains tax liability. The disposal to a company would trigger the liability and this may put them off going down this route were it not for a certain relief. To be completely practical it is necessary to have some confidence that the activity of property investment amounts to a 'business'. This is because, in the right circumstances, transferring properties to a company would qualify for a form of rollover relief. Without that rollover relief capital gains would crystallise as we have identified.

A Property Letting Business?

It may be taken as read that HM Revenue & Customs will rarely if ever accept that property letting is a 'trade'. It therefore cannot attract the crucial inheritance tax business property relief mentioned in chapter 17 or capital gains tax business holdover reliefs. This effectively means that property businesses are generally fully exposed to inheritance tax without further planning and certainly cannot benefit from business gift relief when being transferred.

Inheritance tax business property relief, for instance, is not available in respect of business assets where the business consists "wholly or mainly of dealing in securities, stocks or shares, land or buildings or making or holding investments".

A recent case, The Trustees of David Zetland Settlement TC 02690, merely confirms what has always been understood. That case concerned the availability of inheritance tax business property relief on the occasion of the trust's ten-year charge. Zetland House was a commercial property divided into several smaller units let on a short-term basis to businesses - typically for a period of between one and five years. The strategy of the business was therefore broadly akin to that of a serviced office. Additional services were made available to tenants, but the tribunal found that while additional services were provided, those services were incidental to the core business of letting property. Therefore, business property relief was not available because it was not a trade. Zetland represents a good authority for everything we have said so far.

However, just because an activity is not a 'trade' does not mean that it cannot be a 'business'. This is crucially important. The relief which a 'business' may hope to attract is rollover relief.

Rollover relief on transfer of business to a company provides relief for capital gains tax purposes where an individual or partnership transfers a business and its assets as a going concern wholly or mainly in exchange for shares issued by a company. The leading case in this area is Ramsay v HMRC which was decided in May 2013.

The Facts of Ramsay

The property business in question consisted of a single investment property: a house converted into ten flats, five of which were occupied at the time. On 16 September 2004, the owners transferred the property, subject to an existing bank loan, to a company in exchange for shares. The profits were returned under self-assessment as income from property and not trading. The taxpayer devoted approximately 20 hours a week to various activities of collecting rents and property and garden maintenance.

The Tribunal Decisions

The First-tier Tribunal was the first to consider the application of Taxation of Chargeable Gains Act 1992 section 162 and capital gains tax rollover relief on the transfer of a property letting 'business' to a company in exchange for shares. The First Tier Tax Tribunal found that while the scale of the activities undertaken was commensurate with the size of the property they did not amount to business activities and so capital gains tax relief was denied.

The taxpayers appealed to the Upper Tier Tribunal.

The Upper Tier Tribunal had to decide if what was transferred by Mrs Ramsay was a business. Although this was a question of fact, the Upper Tier Tribunal considered that the First-tier Tribunal had come to its finding based on an error of law.

In the decision, the Judge says,

"in my judgment the word 'business' in the context of s162 TCGA should be afforded a broad meaning. Regard should be had to the factors referred to in Lord Fisher, which in my view (except for the specific references to taxable supplies, which are relevant to VAT) are of general application to the question whether the circumstances describe a business. Thus, it falls to be considered whether (the) activities were a 'serious undertaking earnestly pursued' or a 'serious occupation', whether the activity was an occupation or function actively pursued with reasonable or recognisable continuity, whether the activity had a certain amount of substance in terms of turnover, whether the activity was conducted in a regular manner and on sound and recognised business principles, and whether the activities were of a kind which, subject to differences of detail, are commonly made by those who seek to profit by them."

Although finding that the activities as a whole satisfied these tests the Upper Tier Tribunal pointed out that there remained the question of degree. The Upper Tier Tribunal did not try to set a boundary but found that the degree of activity in this case outweighed what might normally be expected to be carried out by a mere passive property investor.

The Implications of Ramsay

Although the decision gives uncertainty as to where the dividing line precisely is, it does recognise that some property letting activities can be of sufficient nature to constitute a business for capital gains tax rollover relief purposes.

HM Revenue & Customs has indicated that it will not appeal against the Upper Tribunal's decision.

The Ramsay case indicates a very strong presumption in favour of certain property activities as constituting a 'business'.

Where a portfolio comprises, say, a dozen residential or commercial properties and accounts for the past few years indicate significant turnover and average expenditure, then taken in the round, this portfolio could therefore be said to be:

A serious undertaking earnestly pursued, and that the activity has substance in terms of turnover.

An activity conducted in a regular manner and on sound and recognised business principles as is evidenced by the business accounts.

An activity of a kind which is commonly made by those seeking to benefit and profit by them.

We are coming full circle to looking at property investment as a business. The reality is that a property investment venture of any size is likely to be a business but to convince HMRC of that you are talking of scale and with an eye on the above points.

The only point potentially against that conclusion might be that HM Revenue & Customs could potentially argue that the owners are not particularly 'actively engaged' in the business. In the case of Edward and Aethelflead they were very much hands on owners.

Where, however, the owners leave the management to others there are two defences to such an argument by HMRC:

Firstly, the argument ignores the commercial reality that many businesses delegate certain functions to specialists. Delegation is not the point, activity is, whether delegated or not.

Secondly, it is likely that the owners are actively engaged in the business to some degree and there is probably considerable time spent in administration, preparing accounting records, reviewing leases and consulting with professionals. It might be useful to list where time is expended by the senior individuals and add that up on an annual basis.

It seems highly likely in any event that the activities represent a genuine 'business' and consequently could qualify for rollover relief if it were decided to incorporate.

The immediate tax effect of incorporation on the 'business' would be:

- No capital gain on transferring property to the new company since the gain is covered by rollover relief.
- The assets would then be deemed to be held within the company at their current market value for tax purposes rather than cost.
- The shares themselves would 'inherit' the current capital gains tax base cost of the assets.

While this is good news one should balance the possibility against the downsides.

For instance, a transfer of an investment property by an individual to a limited company is normally a chargeable transfer for stamp duty land tax purposes if the previous owner and the company are considered to be connected for tax purposes which the generally will be. SDLT would be payable based on the market value of the properties transferred. For some the SDLT is just a necessary inconvenience to obtain the business structure they want. For others it will weigh against a decision to incorporate. There is no right or wrong answer.

For Edward and Aethelflaed the decision was not to incorporate their existing business but to run subsequent acquisitions through a newly formed company. It was more about flexibility than obsessing over the optimum tax position.

Retaining some property outside of the company meant that they would effectively straddle two separate tax regimes, one corporate and one personal, and they felt that would offer better resilience should the rules change for one regime. One can always count on adverse regime change in taxation! As it turned out they felt that it was good to have property in personal names as the income from those properties did not suffer from the potential restrictions on extractions from companies from 6 April 2016 but that it was also good to have property in a company for the loan interest position and the lower rates of taxation.

What will happen if landlords decide that instead of passing on the business, they would rather sell off their properties. If they have incorporated successfully, the cash that remains after property disposals and corporation tax has been paid, will then be required by the shareholders. If they subsequently withdraw this cash pool from the company, they will incur additional income tax, if not capital gains tax charges. Taken together, these corporation tax and extraction tax costs could possibly exceed the tax costs of a similar, but unincorporated, property business. If that is your real strategy, then it is best to be clear in your own mind and those of your family that this is the case.

A Word on Loans

When considering incorporation we have been looking at property portfolios with no or little debt.

If there is considerable debt then it is questionable whether incorporation is what you need since the debt will reduce the value of the portfolio for inheritance tax purposes as things stand. Most wishing to incorporate while carrying significant debt tend to be more interested in saving income tax and so are really interested in a more personal investment company based strategy.

The problems related to such a strategy are likely to include a need to refinance everything, transferring legal title and the SDLT implications.

A 'beneficial interest company trust' may be used to retain the legal title and mortgage debt in the name of the individual. Essentially, this involves a declaration of trust and an agreement appointing the individual as the company agent in making the mortgage repayments in accordance with the debt delegated to it. Bear in mind though that HMRC may not necessarily agree that the arrangement achieves this outcome.

The mortgage debt has not been legally novated, and it is a moot point whether it is possible to assign the burden of the contract with the mortgage lenders to the company. There may therefore be issues with the treatment of interest payments on the mortgages. Is there really a loan relationship between the company and the mortgage providers that would allow a deduction of the interest payments as non-trading loan relationship debts? Is the payment by the company of the liability remaining with the individuals subject to PAYE deductions as the settlement of a pecuniary liability or is it a capital cost of acquisition?

For those interested in inheritance tax mitigation it is probably not worth overthinking such issues as they are in the game for the medium- longer term and have family wealth at the centre of their concern. It makes no sense at all to risk the valid deductions (against assets for inheritance tax purposes and against income for income tax purposes) for loans in their unincorporated property portfolio.

These questions are more pertinent for those who seek to minimise their income tax liability in the short term by any means and so are beyond the scope of this book.

Chapter 17 - Business Property Relief?

With inheritance tax planning increasingly hampered by anti-avoidance legislation making the most of available reliefs and exemptions is essential for anyone serious about saving this tax.

In this context, business property relief is especially important not only because it can provide relief from the inheritance tax charge on death at up to 100% that is, that is it eliminates the effect of inheritance tax, but also because the scope of the relief is so wide.

The problem for those holding property as an investment is that a business of "property dealing" does not qualify for relief. However, a business of "property development" does qualify for the relief. That may seem an arbitrary distinction but what the legislation, and HMRC, are attempting to do is distinguish a trade which involves land and property from one which merely invests in land and property. They are not the same thing.

So, what is the point in raising the issue of business property relief if property investors can never qualify for it? The answer is that, in the right circumstances and with a determined strategy, it is possible to qualify. If you can achieve and maintain that status, no other planning is required. It is therefore important that you are at least aware of the possibility.

The essential point to grasp is that most people involved in trading, the very characteristic that entitles you to business property relief, never really exploit the relief to its full capacity and some even fail to attract the relief at all. How can that be?

While HMRC may accept that a legitimate trade exists in specific circumstances they may equally adopt the view that most of the business is one of investment rather than of trading and so the whole business including the trading part fails to attract the relief where circumstances allow them to. I have seen HMRC take the point, and sometimes successfully, with engineering companies, medical clinics and builders to name but a few sectors. This tainting of trading status is something which gradually happens over many years as assets accumulate from successful trading so that the investment side in terms of the assets themselves and the income generated by them begins to predominate. The transition may not be so easy to detect for the participants since it happens slowly and organically.

Furthermore, even if HMRC accept that a legitimate trade exists and even predominates, they will always try to maintain that certain assets are not actually being used for business purposes and so cannot attract the relief even though the business itself will. The official term for this unfortunate condition is 'excepted assets'. Even if the requirements for business property relief are met individual assets will be denied relief as 'excepted assets' if they are neither used 'wholly or mainly' for the purposes of the business, nor are required at the date of the owner's death for the future use of the business.

Prime examples of excepted assets include surplus cash within a business, investment properties or a property owned by the business but occupied, say, by the transferor as his or her home.

Property is not relevant business property if the business consists wholly or mainly of dealing in securities, stocks or shares or buildings, or making or holding investments. Investment businesses are therefore denied business property relief.

In contrast, businesses which carry on both investment and trading activities will qualify for relief if they are mainly trading. In practice this tends to be most trading businesses which have some sort of mix. But what is the meaning of "mainly" in the context of trading and investment?

Quantitatively, the test is clear: it means more than 50%. Thus, a business which is 51% trading will attract relief but a business which is 49% trading will attract no relief at all.

Qualitatively, the test is much less clear as there is no statutory guidance. It is unsurprising, therefore, that the application of this 'wholly or mainly' test has spawned several tax cases in recent years.

In the past, the HMRC sought to place great emphasis upon net profitability as being the determining yardstick, so that only those businesses which generated more than 50% of their net profit from trading activities qualified for relief. This approach led to a detailed analysis of the source and nature of the income but also, and this was not always easy to determine, the income against which that expenditure should be deducted.

Despite this approach, a Special Commissioner's decision in Farmer and another (executors of Farmer, deceased) v Inland Revenue Commissioners [1999] STC (SCD) 321 consolidated what has become known as the "in the round" approach. The facts in this case were briefly that the deceased, who died in 1997, left a 449-acre working farm which included many properties which were surplus to the requirements of the farm and were therefore let to third parties. The executors claimed business property relief on the let properties on the basis that there was a single business. HMRC took the view that the net profit position meant that the entire business was an investment business.

The Special Commissioner, however, held that it was necessary to stand back and to consider the business in the round and identified five factors. Of the five relevant factors:

- the overall context of the business;
- the capital employed;
- the time spent by the employees;
- the turnover;
- and the profit

Four, namely, the overall context of the business, the capital employed, the time spent by the employees and consultants and the levels of turnover, all supported the conclusion that the business consisted mainly of farming. The profit figures, and more particularly the net profit figures, on the other hand, supported the opposite view.

Taking the whole business in the round, and without giving predominance to any one factor, the conclusion of the Commissioners was that the business consisted mainly of farming and not of making or holding investments. This 'in the round' type of analysis is now accepted and applied by HMRC.

Property Developers

Generally, property developers, construction companies, are rarely (but surprisingly) interested in inheritance tax business property relief. To a tax specialist that seems counter intuitive but it is nevertheless largely true.

Why is that?

These are very often very successful companies with the founder driving things forward just as resolutely as when the business was in its start-up phase. The mindset therefore tends to be one of generating maximum income and keeping expenditure (which can be immense) and tax completely nailed to the ground and minimised rather than of strategically growing the business. While that is essential in the early years, growing businesses usually require different skills once they reach a certain turnover and profit level if they are to capitalise on the real opportunities available to them. It is not unusual to see a business outstrip the mindset of its owner. The owner works hard and rarely has the time to spare for reflecting on tax strategy and so instinctively regards professional fees for planning as something to be avoided. Income tax or corporation tax is, of course, something to be avoided at all costs and so one often sees huge amounts of value building up in construction companies. Remuneration and dividends tend to be kept down which in turn make the company vulnerable to the charge of holding excepted assets or even disqualifying their whole business on their deaths. It is often only where these companies have grown to the point where it has become necessary to appoint a competent finance director that the issue is constantly drawn to the owners attention and some time is eventually found to devote to the issue. An issue which could ultimately threaten the existence of the company itself and incur hundreds of thousands or even millions in inheritance tax!

The astute reader will see that these business owners have actively chosen to transform their trading businesses, which should attract 100% business property relief and consequently no inheritance tax on their deaths, into little more than personal investment companies which are partly or completely exposed to inheritance tax. While you might believe that to be crazy and the outcome of appalling business management from the perspective of inheritance tax planning (and you would be correct), it is a commonplace outcome which follows from the tunnel vision of many owners. One often finds that professional advisers will go along with this strategy for fear of placing strains on the client relationship or because they simply don't know any better. You will generally get the professional adviser you deserve! What taxpayers actually require are advisers who tell them what they need to know not what they want to hear ... whatever the consequences for their client relationship.

Sometimes that value which compromises the relief lies in investment property portfolios which, although ostensibly investment assets, can be structured as a separate business within the company. Why? Why would you do that?

Investments held by a company are not inevitably excepted assets. They may be used "for the purposes of the business" (American Leaf Co v Director-General 1979) and in the right circumstances constitute an "investment business" within the trading company. The wording of Inheritance Tax Act 1984 section 105(3) confirms that there is such a thing as an "investment business" and if the overall business is not mainly one of holding investments within section 105(3), that value is not excluded from business property relief. It is crucial that one is considering something more than an investment asset. A single property, however valuable, will struggle to qualify as a business. Several investment properties let residentially or commercially are more likely to constitute a letting business. This is something we looked at in the last chapter with that crucial Tax Tribunal decision.

Obviously, the strategy could have a severe impact on any entrepreneurs' relief on the shares. However, for a family construction company to be ultimately continued by the children in due course, entrepreneurs' relief may not be an issue. If the owner is comfortable in this respect the only point to watch is that the value of the investment portfolio does not swamp the trading activity causing the company to be one which is wholly or mainly involved in holding investments, thus bringing section 105(3) into play.

The point is that one could have a company which is trading on 60% of its indicators and yet 40% of the value is in an investment property business. The whole amount will qualify for business property relief.

'So what? I am still a property investor!', you may reasonably say.

The point is that this works equally in reverse, of course. If you currently have a property investment business but have strayed into property development, or would consider doing so, why not increase the activity on the development front to the extent that it swamps the investment side of the business?

A couple of examples which I have witnessed in the last year by way of example.

The first involves an extremely successful property investor who had accumulated a portfolio worth many millions. All totally exposed to inheritance tax! In discussions it transpired that he had started what could be classified as development projects and felt that his new interest could indeed become the dominant side of the business over the next five years or so. So much so that he is now working towards that end. He will retain and expand his property portfolio but maybe less so than he would otherwise have done. It will require constant monitoring and annual meetings, changes to the company articles and new shareholders agreement together with perseverance but these are small things for someone who can see a four million inheritance tax liability as things stand. At age 46 it can only get much worse.... or very much better. If successful that liability could fall to, well, zero.

The second is more modest. A property investment company holding half a dozen properties. During the discussion a copy of the company accounts were produced. Nothing unusual there, the properties were all in fixed assets as one would expect for instance but for one thing. The name of the company which ended in 'Construction Limited.' It turned out on enquiry that the owner had been a builder for 25 years but had now recently turned towards investment. It was a relatively easy matter for him to move back to property development while retaining his investment properties and, with the firm's history, it will be no time at all before his company is mainly a trading company once again. All he needs to do is ensure that the property investment side of things is demonstrably run as a separate business but one which does not predominate (with the Farmer case in mind) within the company. His potential inheritance tax bill will have fallen from £375,000 to zero as a result.

The Property Development Company

For those who would like a little more meat on the bones here are the basic technical underpinnings for those who could potentially benefit from this strategy.

The Legislation

The two types of business, investment and trade, have been clearly distinguished in other legislation. For instance, the EIS legislation distinguishes between "property dealing" (section 297(2)(a)) and "property development" (section 297(2) of the Income and Corporation Tax Act 1988).

The Treasury Statement

Significant non-statutory support for the position was given in answer to a question in Standing Committee E considering the 1976 Finance Bill (HC Official Report 30 June 1976, cols 1268, 1269). The then Chief Secretary to the Treasury Mr Joel Barnett said that business property relief applies on the transfer of a property dealing or property holding business, provided the business includes building construction or land development, and gave a further assurance that the housing stocks of a building company would qualify if regarded as stock in trade.

This makes sense, of course. Think of the big housebuilders. They are all trading and obviously so.

The nature of the business at the time of the transfer or death is critical. A business which started as a house builder but which at the time of the transfer had not built any houses recently and was selling off its land bank may not qualify for relief.

HMRC's Own Manuals IHTM Paragraph 25266.

Building and Construction Companies

"The rule excluding investment businesses from business relief applies to businesses consisting wholly or mainly of dealing in land or buildings. However, this restriction does not deny relief for shares in a company which at the time of the transfer is carrying on a genuine building and construction business holding several properties (e.g. houses or plots awaiting development) as stock in trade."

Case Law

Exors of D Piercey (Decd) v HMRC June 2008 SpC

A development company with rental income from unsold properties. The properties were located in stock not fixed assets. It was found that business property relief was available.

Personal Representatives of McClean Decd v HMRC April 2008 SpC

It was found that a letting of property can be a business but that s.105(3) operates to determines that it is an investment business.

The opportunity is there for those property investors with the right circumstances who can change and manage those circumstances and recognise the opportunity as part of a long-term strategy! Your accountant should be your first port of call here, of course.

Part V – How to Start Planning Effectively

Chapter 18 - How to Start Planning Effectively

Doing nothing is often the worst strategy of all for inheritance tax planning but it is almost always the easiest to implement and, in the short term at least, is generally pain free. That is why it is the most commonly encountered strategy in practice. It is also a strategy of which HM Revenue & Customs wholeheartedly approve for obvious reasons. You will appreciate from the preface and the early chapters that there are usually two major obstacles to undertaking planning – loss of control and a latent capital gains tax liability which will crystallise on any gifts of property.

There is actually a third obstacle, time. In general people are understandably very averse to incurring a tax liability where there is no immediate need to do so. This means that in practice transfers of interests in property are deferred indefinitely. The only alternative visible strategy for many people is to gift property interests in tranches so that gains are covered by the individual's capital gains tax annual exemption (currently £12,000). That strategy is impractical where significant gains are involved. The examples contained in this book suggest this strategy may take several decades or even over a hundred years to fully wash out the gain in many cases.

That additionally assumes that people are going to have the focus and discipline to execute such a strategy year on year, obtaining proper valuations and ensuring that the gift is perfected every time. It is time consuming and precise work. It can work well with modest gains but once one is going beyond two or three years, my experience is that interest in the project begins to dramatically wane. Once the inherent gain is above the £40,000 level this method of dealing with the issue therefore starts to become impractical. Aethelraed could have transferred his property in tranches over five years without incurring any capital gains tax at all but he did not. He could also have paid £53,000 tax if he had transferred the property in one go but he did not even though that sum was peanuts in comparison to what the family eventually paid in inheritance tax.

Remember the importance of having a long - term strategy and a focus on family rather than on 'what's in it for me?' That you are a custodian, a steward, and that you are considering a real legacy to your wider family. This is where the trust comes into play. If you have the vision to use a trust, then capital gains are no longer an obstacle. Neither is the control issue. What you do lose is ownership and that can be the real issue for many people. If you cannot face losing ownership, then you will struggle with inheritance tax planning. The property remains in your estate one way or another. Either it never leaves your estate, or, through half-hearted planning, it is caught by the gift with reservation of benefit rules.

If there is no capital gains tax problem because you are about to acquire or have just acquired a property (so its acquisition cost equates to its current market value for capital gains tax purposes) then this would be a good time to consider a property income trust or a family investment company to hold it, other things being equal. If capital gains tax is an issue, then a trust should be at the top of your shopping list or alternatively consider some of the ways of changing the nature of the asset gifted and outlined in chapters 7 - 9.

Given that in practice property portfolio's represent the most common asset class which is hammered by inheritance tax every year, an immediate charge to capital gains tax and fretting about asset protection is very rarely an adequate reason for doing nothing when it can be deftly side-stepped by anyone in the position of Aethelraed and Alfred.

As well as adopting a practical mindset as far as possible one must take two steps:

STEP 1

The first step in avoiding Aethelraed's mistake is to have a precise understanding of the inheritance tax position on your (hypothetical at this stage, of course) death. Property, investments and savings, business interests, everything. Know what you would pay if you died today. This requires a one-page calculation. Without it you cannot proceed.... effectively.

STEP 2

The second step in avoiding Aethelraed's mistake is to have a precise understanding of the current capital gains tax position if you made a gift of any property today ... while you are very much alive and in control of the position.

Exact and precise accurate figures supported by documentation is what is required. Not abstractions but detailed information on each property including professional valuations.

Know exactly what the capital gains tax and inheritance tax liabilities would be as well as the anticipated growth in value and you are completely in control. If you cannot write these things down, you cannot proceed.... Effectively in any event.

To seriously take these two essential steps you therefore need to be absolutely clear on:

1. The current market value of your assets today, especially your properties.

2. The dates of acquisition of your properties and their original cost as well as the dates and cost of any improvements over the years.

3. Your wishes, concerns and family circumstances. My experience is that this is best achieved by what might be called a focussed' brain dump'. Schedule a morning or afternoon in peace and quiet and note everything down on a first draft. What you are looking for at the end of the session is a single A4 sheet with a clear statement on these matters. This sounds straightforward but it is also quite difficult because you are forcing yourself to write down what may have been little more than tentative musings and the occasional passing thought until now. Giving them physical form is important. If this process takes you more than a couple of hours and/or your final sheet exceeds a single sheet of paper, you need to start again ... and relax.

If you find yourself unable to gather your thoughts in this way, I would suggest that you are not yet ready to embark on the journey. You need to reflect some more on what is important to you.

4. Be honest with yourself about your mindset. You may genuinely prefer to hold on to ownership until the bitter end.... and that is fine, but you and your family should recognise the fact and the implications. The price for retaining ownership of everything is the inheritance tax the family will suffer.

5. Be honest about the mindset of your professional advisers. Have a look at Chapter 9 (Your Adviser's Mindset) of my companion book, 'The Absolute Essence of Inheritance Tax Planning' You need someone who can think like you do and this book tells you what to look for and how to find it in your adviser.

Aethelraed saw trust planning as an exercise in self-indulgence and entertainment.

Alfred by contrast saw it as a means to an end. If trust planning could not help him achieve that end it was nothing more than a distraction.

It is possible to understand and empathise with both Aethelraed and Alfred but which character you are drawn towards will determine your success, or lack of it, with inheritance tax planning with respect to investment property.

Whether you have a single investment property or several hundred, the only limit to the depth and reach of your inheritance tax planning with respect to investment property is your ambition.

Thank You

Before we part company, I would like to say a sincere "thank you" for purchasing my book and reading all the way through it to the end. If you have found this book useful I should be extremely grateful if you would take a minute or two of your time to leave a review on Amazon. It means a lot. Thank you.

No book I have ever read is perfect and this one is no exception. If there are any oversights, omissions or errors or anything you would like to see covered or changed, please email me at stevesbooks@gmail.com.

About the Author

Steve is a practicing UK tax adviser with over 35 years experience, a writer and blogger.

He believes that words can change the way people see the world, their mindset, and that this can have profound consequences.

Mindset may be defined as a particular way of thinking, a person's attitude or inclination about something. Change this, even slightly, and the world becomes a different place.

Appendix I – Tax & Formal Trusts

Income Tax and Capital Gains Tax

Any dividends will be taxed at the Schedule F trust rate of 38.1%.

Other, non-dividend, income will be taxed at 45%.

If the trustees decide to pay that income to a beneficiary, the beneficiary is taxed on the income received but can offset the tax paid by the trustees against that liability. This means that beneficiaries who are non-taxpayers or basic rate taxpayers will probably be due repayments of tax where income is regularly paid out to them.

To the extent that the trust has paid more tax on that income that the beneficiary would be required to pay, that additional tax can be reclaimed from the Revenue by the beneficiary. However, due to a mismatch between the taxation of dividends and the taxation of the discretionary trust, the income tax treatment can be disadvantageous if the trustees receive a significant level of dividend income. This disadvantage can be managed, but it is a complex area.

Capital gains realised in the trust are taxed at the trust rate of 28% on residential property and 20% on other assets, subject to the trust annual exemption (2019/20 - £6,000). Where assets are passed out to beneficiaries the capital gain can usually be held over.

Inheritance Tax

The Ten-Year Anniversary Charge

Trusts are subject to an inheritance tax charge on every tenth anniversary of their creation

The thinking behind the legislation is to subject a relevant property trust to inheritance tax as if the property in the settlement had been the subject of a lifetime gift made every generation. The rate of inheritance tax on death is 40%, whereas the rate on chargeable lifetime gifts (which the donor survives by more than seven years) is 20%. A generation is assumed to be 33 1/3 years. HMRC understandably want to collect the money rather more regularly than three times every 100 years, so the charge on property in the settlement is collected every ten years at a maximum rate of 6%, which equates to 20% every 33 1/3 years. However, 6% is a maximum rate and in most cases the effective rate will be much less than this, given the effect of the nil-rate band for each trust.

The Exit Charge

This charge arises when property leaves the relevant property regime, by way of appointment out of the trust. There is no exit charge if the event happens in the first quarter (three months) following either creation of the settlement or the last ten-year anniversary. If the trust was established by will, there is no exit charge if the event happens within two years, but at least three months, after the death. There is a distinction between calculation of the exit charge in the first ten years of the life of the settlement and the ten-year period following the first or subsequent ten-year anniversaries. The exit charge in the first ten years is related back to the circumstances at the date of settlement (subject to scaling down to reflect the number of three month periods or quarters which have elapsed since then). If there was no positive charge to inheritance tax at outset, there will generally be no charge on an exit within the first ten years, whatever the then value of the property.

However, in calculating the rate of tax on an exit within the first ten years in a case where business or agricultural property went into the settlement, note that the initial deemed chargeable transfer is the gross and not the net value. The exit charge following the first ten-year anniversary adopts the rate charged on the last anniversary, again scaled down by reference to the number of completed quarters

On a subsequent disposal of the trust assets, the trust would normally be taxed at 20% or 28% depending on the nature of the asset on any gain it makes after accounting for the available annual exemption.

Appendix II: The Structure of Company Share Capital

The Share Capital

One of the first things to consider when structuring a family investment company are the share rights. The articles of association set out exactly what share capital a company has and what rights attach to such shares. The three main types of shares are ordinary shares, preference shares or redeemable shares.

All companies must have some ordinary share capital and if model articles are adopted the ordinary shares would have an equal right to voting, income and capital. This is most companies. If bespoke articles are adopted, the rights can be tailored to meet the objectives of the company. This is most family investment companies.

Preference shares are shares that have enhanced rights to income and/or capital. The rights tend to come before other shares classes.

Redeemable shares are shares that have rights to be redeemed generally at their par value. Issuing redeemable shares can be useful for a family investment company as it creates a convenient mechanism to return capital to shareholders. Redeemable shares do not have to carry any rights to interest.

A share is a bundle of rights made up of rights to vote, income and capital. The rights attaching to different types of shares can be drafted in many ways and it may be helpful to consider each of those rights in turn.

Rights to Vote

If control of a family investment company is managed through the rights given to its directors, the right to vote attaching to shares becomes less important. If one takes the view that simplicity is always best, then most ordinary shares would be given an equal right to vote.

Consideration should be given to the different levels of control and influence that voting rights give shareholders.

They are:

75% or more of the shares, gives shareholders total control as they have the right to pass special resolutions. This covers the right to adopt new articles of association and therefore the power to completely change a company's rule book;

50% or more but less than 75% of the shares, gives shareholders the power to pass an ordinary resolution. This covers the rights to appoint or dismiss directors;

25% or more but less than 50% of the shares, gives shareholders the power to block a special resolution. Often referred to as an influential minority holding; and

Less than 25% of the shares is an uninfluential minority, that arguably gives the shareholders little real power in the company.

It might be suggested that in order to manage control of a family investment company, it is helpful to have voting and non-voting shares. Those wishing to retain control but not value, say for inheritance tax purposes, may be tempted to hold voting shares but gift shares with just income and capital rights (but with no voting rights) to children and grandchildren. Such an approach requires caution however, as it is likely that HMRC will regard the voting shares as retaining significant value even without income and capital rights. The rationale HMRC will adopt is that by having the voting rights, such shareholders can simply change the articles of the company to give themselves income and/or capital.

Rights to Income

Consider the income rights which should be given to each type of share.

Generally, ordinary shares will have a right to income. Be careful to avoid shares that only have a right to income given these shares may be caught by the settlement's legislation (see appendix VII). Preference shares tend to have a special right to income and may be useful if you have a shareholder that needs income ahead of others.

The Use of 'Alphabet' Shares

The flexibility of paying dividends to different shareholders at different times can appear very attractive. Dividend waivers can enable some flexibility, but they rely on the shareholder deciding not to take a dividend which is perhaps not attractive in a family investment company situation where it is normally desirable for the board of directors to have control over the payment of dividends.

In order to obtain flexibility, it is therefore preferable to issue different classes of shares. Their rights may mirror each other, but as a separate class, the directors can declare dividends at different rates and times.

The use of alphabet shares does come with the real risk of challenge by HMRC under the settlements legislation where as a result of the arrangements a spouse or minor child may benefit. If dividends are paid to one class of shares to the determent of other classes, there is a risk of a capital gains tax value shift. If a parent has shares in a family investment company and gives shares to his or her children, but then uses his or her powers to pay dividends on just his or her shares to the determent of the other share classes, it may be argued by HMRC that he or she has retained a benefit.

One possible solution to the risk of challenge is to limit the rights attaching to each class of shares so that they can only receive dividends up to their proportionate share in the distributable reserves. Such restrictions can and should be included in the articles of association.

Rights to Capital

Capital rights can all be equal, or you can create shares that will have enhanced rights to capital, generally called growth shares. Redeemable shares will tend to have a preferred right to capital so that they are repaid ahead of the ordinary shares.

Growth shares have an enhanced right to capital with the result that the growth in value of the company passes to those shares in place of other shares whose value is effectively frozen. The capital rights may accumulate from incorporation or after the company's value has reached a certain hurdle. The shares are useful as they can freeze the value of shares retained by parents allowing all the capital growth of the company to flow to the children. An excellent inheritance tax strategy which is discussed in chapter 15.

The existence of growth shares does complicate a structure and will make valuing the shares more difficult. If, for income purposes, different classes of shares are to be established, it can be helpful to give each class of share slightly different rights to capital. This helps to ensure that each class of share is actually treated as a separate class. Shares which purport to be different classes by description only, for instance by calling them ordinary A shares and Ordinary B shares etc, but which otherwise have identical rights, may end up being classified by HMRC as a single class.

Limited or Unlimited?

A family investment company may be formed as either a limited or an unlimited company. By using an unlimited company, the family investment company will benefit from an exemption to file accounts at Companies House, keeping the family's finances a little more private. It is worth remembering that the articles of association, details of shareholders, directors and people with significant control are all publicly available.

An unlimited company will remain liable for its debts if the company has enough assets to meet its liabilities. Provided the family investment company is only used to hold investments it should never have liabilities in excess of its assets.

If the family investment company intends to trade or acquire any assets, such as a property, which carry risks that could exceed its assets, then it is sensible to use a limited company. Provided the company was originally set up as unlimited, it can convert to limited status and vice versa but a company can only convert one way once. If an unlimited company is preferred it is advisable to form the company as unlimited so that the option to convert to limited liability status, should the nature of the business change, remains open.

An unlimited company also benefits from less onerous obligations under the Companies Act 2006 should it wish to return capital to shareholders.

If an unlimited company becomes the parent company of a limited company, then it losses its exemption to file accounts at Companies House.

Appendix III - Control and Management

The Articles of Association

The articles of association of a company represent the internal rule book and the latest version must always be filed at Companies House making them publicly available. They set out how the company appoints and dismisses its directors, how directors manage the company, the duties of the directors, what share capital it can issue, share rights and restrictions and how shareholders meetings operate.

Under the Companies Act 2006, model articles provide the basic approach for a limited company, but a company is free to adopt its own bespoke articles subject to certain limitations under the Companies Act 2006. A family investment company will invariably adopt bespoke articles. This can prove extremely useful when considering long term inheritance tax planning. Articles can either be in short form, setting out just how they differ from the model articles or long form, where they set out the full rules applying to the company. Long form is a convenient way to ensure that all the rules are in one place. There are no model articles for an unlimited company.

A key limitation is that a company must not deprive itself or fetter its ability to alter its articles by any arrangements contained in its articles. Articles can be amended with 75% shareholder approval. It is possible however for the shareholders to contract between themselves for different rules to apply.

It is best to include important powers and restrictions in the articles as the legal remedies for breach are more effective than the remedies for breach of contract under a shareholders' agreement. For example, it is possible to obtain an injunction to stop a course of action that is in breach of the articles. Whereas the remedy for a breach under a shareholders' agreement is normally in the form of damages.

The Shareholders' Agreement

A shareholders' agreement is generally held to be a legally binding contract between the shareholders and usually the company, whereby the parties agree on matters relating to the operation of the company. A shareholders' agreement is a private document, so it is better to include personal family matters in this document rather than the articles which are public. Under a shareholders' agreement, the shareholders can agree how they will exercise their voting rights in certain situations. For example, the shareholders can agree that they will not use their votes to amend the articles, issue shares, appoint directors etc without the board's prior approval to such action. This may be appropriate where the directors are to have more day to day control.

Alternatively, if its desirable for the shareholders to have more control, the shareholders' agreement can set out matters which limit the boards power. For example, the board of directors may be required to obtain shareholder approval before issuing more shares, making large investments or disposals. Often referred to as "reserved matters" the shareholder can limit the scope of the board of directors' powers. Where a shareholders' agreement exists, the articles will generally make the signing of a deed of adherence to the shareholders' agreement a pre-condition before being entered into the register of members of a company. This ensures that new shareholders must agree to the terms of the shareholders' agreement.

Every family investment company should have shareholders agreement.

Most companies do not have a shareholder agreement.

The Board of Directors

Where a family investment company is established for estate and inheritance tax planning purposes, the founders are normally looking to get as much value out of their estates as possible while maintaining control over the assets. A classic inheritance tax strategy.

In light of this, the founders may not want to have any shares in their own names if possible, given that shares represent ownership and therefore value in the company. Therefore, to retain control, the founders will be directors of the company and will look to have as much power as possible transferred to the board of directors. When drafting the articles of association, consideration should be given to several specific points. The number of directors and whether there should be a limit on numbers, whether adult children should be directors, how many directors are needed for a meeting to be quorate, who will be the chairman, and should they have a casting vote, is a decision of the majority of directors appropriate and could you have a deadlock situation?

Under the model articles board appointments can be made by ordinary resolution or by the board. It can be helpful to consider if others should have the power to appoint board members, for example if husband and wife are the only directors, what would happen if they die together? It may not be desirable for the shareholders as a group to decide on the next board of directors. To address this concern, it is possible to give some shareholders embedded rights to appoint board members. If a family trust owns some shares in the family investment company, for instance, the trustees may be given these powers and the founders can leave instructions to the trustees on who should be appointed.

These issues become particularly important if the company is to have only one director. Even though it is quite common in practice, it is suggested that having a sole director is not to be encouraged.

Using Trusts

When considering control of a company, trusts can be a very useful tool indeed.

Where a trust owns shares in a family investment company, the trustees will have voting rights which can be useful. Trustees can be given embedded rights for example to appoint board members, which may be exercised if the board is wiped out in family disaster. It does happen!

Minors should not own shares in their own name but, if they do, they cannot vote or agree to sell or transfer shares. Minor's shares should be held in a bare trust. The shares may be transferred to them when they turn 18, but (provided the articles include appropriate provisions) before any new shareholder can be entered in the register of members, they must first sign a deed of adherence to any existing shareholders agreement.

Trusts also have other uses. They can represent an additional shareholder, which is very helpful if the intention is that each shareholder has a minority interest to reduce the value of each holding. They provide flexibility to deliver income to a non-shareholder or additional income to an existing shareholder that may only have a small shareholding and so does not have sufficient income rights. For example, a flexible discretionary trust can receive a dividend from the family investment company and then pay the income to anyone in the class of beneficiaries.

Trusts are also very useful as a means of holding shares for unborn family members. For example, a family investment company set up for grandchildren may work very efficiently for estate planning purposes, but what happens when a new grandchild is born? If a trust has some shares, those shares can be passed to the grandchild or rather a bare trust for their benefit without a tax charge due to the benefit of capital gains tax holdover relief. Without a trust, the grandparents would have to fund the subscription for more shares, but they may not have the funds to do so and the cost may be expensive if the family investment company has grown significantly in value since incorporated.

The Control of Dividend Payments

In order to pay a dividend, a company must have sufficient distributable reserves. Distributable reserves are normally calculated by reference to the company's last accounts, but interim accounts can be prepared to demonstrate that sufficient reserves are available. Typically, the board of directors are entitled to declare and pay interim dividends and will

recommend a final dividend to shareholders after the end of an accounting period. It is possible however to give the directors sole responsibility to declare dividends in the articles of association.

Share Transfers

The articles of association will generally set out the procedure for share transfers. In a family investment company, it is appropriate to have very bespoke share transfer provisions. All share transfers can be subject to board approval, although some exceptions for permitted transfers are common.

The permitted transfers that may be appropriate for a family investment company are transfers to family members (but excluding spouses and civil partners); and trusts for family members.

It is worth considering extending the definition of a family trust to include trusts established in a will on the death of a shareholder giving the surviving spouse a life interest. This will secure inter-spouse relief, avoiding an inheritance tax charge on the value of the shares. The trustees of such a trust can be given instructions to ensure that the shares come back to family members either on the death of the surviving spouse or earlier.

If transfers to family trusts are permitted, the board of directors should be given powers to approve the trustees. Trustees will have the right to exercise the voting rights, so it is appropriate that the board have some discretion to vet the trustees.

In addition to permitted transfers, provisions may also be included in the articles to deal with the compulsory transfer of shares on certain milestone events, such as death, bankruptcy and/or divorce. Compulsory transfer provisions can also apply if a shareholder is in breach of any rules.

Under the compulsory transfer provisions, the board normally have the power to determine when they wish to trigger the provisions. If they do, the board can determine what happens to the shares. The company could buy them back (if permitted to do so and it has the distributable reserves); another family member or family trust may purchase the shares; or the shares may be offered around the other shareholders.

The articles would normally include a procedure for agreeing the price the shares are purchase for, normally this would be the open market value taking account of the size of holding, and the procedure for the purchase of the shares.

Appendix IV - Asset Protection

A key objective of estate planning is to protect wealth for future generations. There are a few risks to family wealth including the impact of taxation, poor investment decisions, bankruptcy and, of course, divorce which all need to be catered for.

A family investment company can provide some protection from all of the above risks. With a 40% rate on the total value of assets, perhaps the biggest tax risk is inheritance tax, and this is addressed by spreading ownership between family members and passing the shares down the generations. A classic inheritance tax strategy. Provided the family investment company is properly managed, its assets will be protected from poor decisions that individual shareholders may otherwise make if they owned the assets personally.

A family investment company cannot prevent a shareholder becoming bankrupt, but at least the articles can include a mechanism to buy the shares back from the trustee in bankruptcy at an open market value, retaining the shares in the family and keeping the assets of the family investment company protected. Similar rules can also apply on divorce, of course.

When a shareholder divorces, the family court will look to all their financial resources to determine what is an appropriate financial settlement. The priority of the court is always going to be the needs of the parties. Shares in a family investment company will definitely be seen as a resource.

If the company has been set up and used for legitimate purposes (e.g. tax efficiency, passing wealth down the generations, general wealth protection) then the corporate veil will generally not be pierced.

However, it will also be necessary to ensure as far as possible that the company controller/shareholder cannot be deemed to have a beneficial interest in the company's assets.

The following certainly would assist in this respect:

Family investment companies involving multiple shareholders (which is of course the norm) offer an additional layer of protection, because the court would find it harder to assign the whole beneficial interest in any property held by the company to only one of the shareholders, given that it would prejudice the other shareholders.

Where the assets are being "introduced" to the company by the family of the company's controller/shareholder, Matrimonial Causes Act section 24(1)(a) cannot apply because it would be the family, and not the shareholder, who would be "entitled" to the property. The family investment company set up in order to protect the following generations from claims on divorce will therefore be protected.

If the company were a trading company rather than a property holding company, it will be far harder to trace current assets back to any initial injection of wealth by the controller/shareholder, and there will be an argument that growth in the value of the company cannot be beneficially owned by the controller/shareholder.

Where the controller/shareholder is introducing the assets to the company, it would be very helpful to have clear corporate documentation regarding where the beneficial interests in those assets lie. This is often missing or incomplete.

It must also be remembered that although the company's assets will be protected, the shareholding would be vulnerable. The following issues would assist in this context.

The company's governance documentation (i.e. the articles of association, but if not then the shareholders agreement) can be drafted to restrict transfers of shareholdings and to include compulsory transfer provisions which set the value of the shares reflecting a discount for a minority interest.

If a trust owns shares in a family investment company, the trust can provide yet another layer of protection in the event of a divorce. Although where a trust is used for protection, care needs to be taken to ensure that it is and remains a 'non-nuptial settlement' as it were since the courts do have power to vary nuptial settlements.

Several factors should be considered, including who are the beneficiaries, what is the purpose of the trust, who are the trustees and are they independent from the beneficiary. If a beneficiary is seen as being able to call upon trust assets as he or she wishes, the courts are more likely to regard the trust as a nuptial settlement.

Where asset protection is important to taxpayers, they should insist on family members have pre or post marital agreements. This is the best way to provide asset protection and could be a requirement set out in the shareholders' agreement. Such agreements will be upheld by the court provided they are considered fair.

Appendix V - Funding Issues for the Family Investment Company

The Options

The source of funds for a family investment company can originate from either share capital or debt. On formation, cash is generally used to provide the family investment company with at least its initial funding. If a company has been established for some years, fresh cash can always be introduced by subscribing for new shares. Having share capital is advantageous for a company and its shareholders. For example, to get the full benefit of discounts for minority interests, it is helpful for the family investment company to have been funded with share capital rather than debt. Debt will not attract a discount like share capital. Share capital also gives a family investment company substance by strengthening its balance sheet, perhaps not as important as for a trading company but it can be helpful if trying to demonstrate that a family investment company has been established with the right intention of operating an investment business for its shareholders. A key advantage of using cash to subscribe for shares is that it triggers no tax charges.

If cash is unavailable, it is possible to sell assets to a family investment company. A sale will trigger a disposal for capital gains tax purposes and either SDLT or stamp duty depending on the asset. Sales of assets are best undertaken for full market value to avoid other tax charges and the sale consideration can be left outstanding as a debt. If it is not desirable to have outstanding debt, then the debt can eventually be capitalised, i.e. exchanged for an issue of shares either by the lender or their assignees.

A gift to a company cannot be a potentially exempt transfer under Inheritance Tax Act 1984 section 3A as such gifts have to be made to an individual (or certain trusts). A gift to a company is treated as a chargeable lifetime transfer. Such gifts will therefore trigger a 20% lifetime charge on the value of the gift (which is strictly the loss to the estate) subject to any applicable exemptions.

It is arguable that if you make the gift at a time when you own 100% of the company, that your estate has not actually been reduced in value and therefore while a chargeable lifetime transfer has occurred the value is nil and therefore the tax is nil. While this may be helpful, the problem then comes when the owner wishes to gift shares to their family to establish a family investment company structure. As the company now has assets that were gifted to it, the shares will stand at a gain, so any gift of shares will probably trigger a capital gains tax disposal.

Using Loans

The funding of a family investment company by way of loans is undoubtedly attractive. Loans are flexible especially when executed as interest free and repayable on demand. However, before deciding on making loans, particularly if loans are the preferred basis for the majority of funding for a family investment company, then careful consideration of the anti-avoidance rules is needed.

HMRC accept that a loan made on interest free, repayable on demand terms does not give rise to a transfer of value for inheritance tax purposes. However, if the loan is not repayable for a fixed period, the value of the loan will be reduced, and a chargeable transfer may arise. For this reason, most loans will always be repayable on demand.

Interest may or may not be charged. The obvious advantage to charging interest is it makes the loan arrangements appear more commercial. This certainly assists with a possible challenge under the settlement's legislation considered further below. It may also assist with a challenge under the transaction in securities rules (appendix VI) as it suggests that the arrangements were not entered into for the purpose of gaining an income tax advantage.

Appendix VI – The Family Investment Company & Transactions in Securities

This represents anti-avoidance legislation which you should be aware of. It broadly seeks to eliminate any income tax advantage which would otherwise be taxable as a dividend or distribution.

HMRC has the power to counteract tax advantages obtained in consequence of one or more transactions in securities where an income tax advantage is sought. The income tax provisions are found in in Income Tax Act 2007, Part 13 Tax Avoidance, Chapter 1 sections 682-703. The transactions in securities regime apples where a person is a party to one or more "transactions in securities" and a person (not necessarily the same person) obtains an income tax advantage in consequence of the transactions. Either Condition A or Condition B must be met and the main purpose or one of the main purposes of the person being involved in the transactions in securities was to obtain the income tax advantage. The rules only apply to close companies. It is also worth noting that the onus rests on HMRC to prove that the transactions in securities regime applies. The definition of a transaction in securities is wide and includes subscribing for shares, altering share rights or returning share capital.

Condition A is that, as a result of the transaction in securities or any one or more of the transactions in securities, a relevant person receives relevant consideration in connection with:

(a) the distribution, transfer or realisation of assets of a close company,

(b) the application of assets of a close company in discharge of liabilities, or

(c) the direct or indirect transfer of assets of one close company to another close company,

and the relevant person does not pay or bear income tax on the consideration.

Relevant consideration means consideration that represents assets which are available for distribution by way of dividend by the close company.

The link between the income tax advantage and the transaction in securities does not have to be direct, it just has to be part of an overall arrangement.

Condition B is that:

(a) a relevant person receives relevant consideration in connection with the transaction in securities or any one or more of the transactions in securities,

(b) two or more close companies are concerned in the transaction or transactions in securities concerned, and

(c) the relevant person does not pay or bear income tax on the consideration.

Is a loan repayment caught by the regime?

The first issue to consider, is whether a loan itself a security for these purposes. Generally, you would think it was not although it may be possible. What is clear however is that the subscription of shares will be a transaction in securities under the regime.

For HMRC to succeed in a challenge on this basis they would have to prove that the subscription for shares was done with the intension of securing an income tax advantage. This may be difficult, especially if the funding for the family investment company took place sometime ago. It may also be difficult if the family investment company received most of its working capital in the form of a share subscription and the loan was not material compared to the overall value of the company. Another strong argument for share subscriptions and not trying to be too clever.

The case law on the strength of connection between the transaction in securities, being the share subscription, and the loan and its repayment does not have to be strong, but it does need to be shown as being all part of the same arrangement.

This may be difficult for HMRC to prove. It may also be argued that the making of a loan to a close company is very common and by virtue of how common it is, it makes the arrangement commercial when perhaps compared with other arrangements such as issuing redeemable preference shares.

The point is to be aware of this anti-avoidance legislation. Many 'lets just say' varieties of tax planning are victims of this legislation. HMRC are well experienced in distinguishing between a convenient story, however well crafted, and what has actually transpired. Tread carefully!

It has to be said that this legislation applies where individual seeking income tax mitigation by re-characterising what would normally be dividends or other distributions without paying income tax on the extractions. Genuine family investment company owners who are seeking inheritance tax mitigation are advised to steer clear of such temptations.

They are not necessary.

Appendix VII - The Family Investment Company & the Settlements Legislation

Yet more anti-avoidance legislation to at least be aware of.

The settlements legislation is found in Income Tax (Trading & Other Income) Act 2005, Part 5, Chapter 5 and applies to trusts, companies, individuals and partnerships. Do not underestimate its importance.

It covers:

Settlor interested trusts;

Settlements for minor children;

Capital sums paid to settlors by a settlement; and

Capital sums paid by a company connected with a settlement.

HMRC guidance on the settlement's legislation can be found in the Trusts, Settlements and Estates Manual paragraph 4001 onwards. It is a useful summary of the rules although obviously reflecting HMRC's interpretation of the legislation.

HMRC's purpose is best summed up in their own Trusts and Estates Manual which states at TSEM paragraph 4015:

"The settlements legislation is intended to prevent an individual from gaining a tax advantage by making arrangements which divert his or her income to another person who is liable at a lower rate of tax or is not liable to income tax. It applies only where the settlor has retained an interest in the settled property or income."

The definition of a settlement is very, very wide and includes any arrangement, trust, disposition or transfer of assets. 'Any arrangement' can include a series of transactions. But in all cases, there must be an element of bounty as established in CIR v Plummer [1979] STC 793. Commercial transactions made at arm's length are outside the scope of the legislation. At TSEM4105, HMRC give an example by way of Jones v Garnett (78 TC 597) the arrangement was the simple issue of a share in a company where the 'bounty' was provided by the expectation of the settlor's subsequent behaviour.

A settlor is someone that has provided the funds either directly or indirectly for the settlement. Let HMRC themselves describe how they see this.

Example taken from TSEM paragraph 4120 – An Indirect Settlor:

"X is the director and owns all the 150 issued ordinary £1 shares of X Ltd. X Ltd issues 100 new ordinary £1 shares which are acquired for £100 by the X Family Trust. The trust has been established for the benefit of X's family by his father, X Senior, who created the trust by settling cash of £100. Shortly after the issue of the new shares, a dividend of £100 per share is declared and paid and the trust receives dividends of £10,000. X controlled the arrangement for the issue of the shares at par [which must have been at a discount in order for the arrangement to include an element of bounty] followed by the dividend. X is therefore the true settlor of the settlement from which income of £10,000 arose. The original settlement of £100 by X Senior is usually disregarded on de-minimis grounds."

Having identified who is a settlor, you then must consider if the settlor has retained an interest. A settlor is deemed to have retained an interest in a trust if "that property or any related property is, or will or may become, payable to or applicable for the benefit of the settlor or his spouse or civil partner in any circumstances whatsoever." An example given in the manual is where shares are gifted to a brother on the basis that the shares will be given back after a dividend has been paid to the brother – TSEM paragraph 4200, example 3.

"A benefit can still arise to the settlor or their spouse, if income is paid to a third party. Where a settlor has retained an interest in a settlement, the income of the settlement will be taxed on the settlor (subject to a few exceptions for certain types of income). There is an important exception to the rule on settlor retained interests, where a settlor has made an outright gift to their spouse or civil partner unless: the gift does not carry a right to the whole of the income, or the property given is wholly or substantially a right to income."

An outright gift cannot be subject to conditions or arrangements whereby the giver can receive the asset back or receive a benefit from it.

Here is an example of a gift which is substantially a right to income (taken from TSEM paragraph 4205, example 5):

"An engineering company has 100 ordinary £1 shares. Mr P and Mr O own 50 ordinary shares each. They create a new class of B shares which carry no voting rights and no assets in a winding up. They then issue 50 B shares to each of their wives. Dividends voted on those B shares would be treated as the income of Mr P and Mr O rather than their wives as the B dividends are from shares that are wholly or substantially a right to income and so not exempted from ITTOIA/S624 by ITTOIAS626. (This example is based on the High Court case of Young v Pearce; Young v Scrutton (1996) STC 743)."

An example of a gift which was not substantially a right to income (taken from TSEM Paragraph 4205 example 6):

"X is an IT consultant. He owns all the shares in a private company through which he sells his services. The company receives all the income he generates. The company's only source of income is from work carried out by X. It has insignificant capital assets. X transfers his shares in the company to his wife by way of gift. His work in one year earns the company more than £70,000 but he decides to draw only £40,000 salary. This leaves £30,000 profit for the company. The company then pays a dividend of £30,000 to Mrs X. The arrangement effectively transfers part of X's earnings to his wife. However, the House of Lords judgment in the case of Jones v Garnett confirmed that the focus of ITTOIA/S626 was the settled property. Regardless of the underlying arrangement the transfer of shares is an outright gift between spouses. Unlike the shares in the example above, the property gifted here is a holding of ordinary shares with rights to capital. The gift is not therefore of property which is wholly or substantially a right to income. The settlements legislation does not apply, and we would not treat the dividend as the income of X."

These two examples from HMRC highlight the different tax result arising from the rights attaching to the shares. In the second example, the shares had rights to income and capital so could not be treated as simply a right to income, whereas in the first example, the shares only had a right to income.

It may be argued that the income arising from the benefit of a loan in the borrower's hands will form part of the total income of the lender under the settlement's legislation. But can a loan be a settlement for the purposes of the settlement's legislation?

As noted, the definition of a settlement is very widely drafted and certainly could include an arrangement to loan money.

Bounty?

Arguably there can be in circumstances where the borrower has the use of the loaned funds and presuming, he or she is not required to pay anything (such as interest) for the use of those funds. If a settlement exists, is it settlor interested? Given the lender has the right to receive the loaned funds back then arguably he has retained an interest in the asset of the settlement.

However, there are arguments that it is not.

Consider again what is the settled property. The lender has arguably merely exchanged the money lent for the right to have the money repaid (a "chose in action") which does not give rise to any income. The lender has no interest in the proceeds of the loan which belong to the borrower.

One useful case with respect to loans is IRC v Levy [1982] STC 442. In this case Mr Levy owned 99% of the shares in a company that dealt in stocks and shares. Mr Levy and his wife made several interest free, repayable on demand loans to the company. HMRC argued that the loans were bounty and that a settlement existed with the result that the income generated by the company on the capital lent to it, should be taxed on Mr Levy.

It was held that the test for determining bounty was subjective, not objective, and the transactions should be looked at as a whole. Mr Levy gave up something, though in circumstances where he anticipated and intended to secure from those transactions a compensating advantage to himself (as majority shareholder). There was found to be no bounty and therefore no settlement.

Appendix VIII - Information Requirements for Estate and Inheritance tax Planning

It is easy to talk in a general sense about inheritance but planning is always, always driven by the individuals circumstances. The following guidelines as to the sort of information and input may prove useful.

A brief note of no more than one to four A4 pages setting out the family circumstances. The note should include details of any concerns or worries as well as the objectives which should be considered.

Information for each spouse or partner:

Date of birth.

Any health issues.

A copy of the latest will(s).

Details of each asset including date of acquisition and cost, date and cost of any enhancement expenditure, current value (along with any professional valuation or basis for valuation), details of legal and beneficial ownership and address and post code if property including the home.

A copy of the latest self-assessment calculation.

Latest accounts for any trading or investment business.

Details of life assurance policies – provider, account number, copy deed.

Details of any loans, mortgages, account numbers, terms, etc.

If you know where you are starting from you stand a very good chance of planning your route to where you want to be. That is minimal exposure to inheritance tax. If your current location is fuzzy and based on unsubstantiated assumptions the likelihood is that any planning will remain a hypothetical exercise only.

Printed in Great Britain
by Amazon